Praise for *The Art of*

Margo Majdi is one of the most powerful and inspirational leaders I've ever known. She is unstoppable in her commitment to people letting go of their limitations. Margo's love for people and ability to see them in their authenticity is second to none. A world-class coach, she is creating a legacy for generations to come. Her book, *The Art of Acknowledgement*, is a must read!

**Michael Strasner**
*Transformational Trainer/Business Coach*
*Best Selling Author, Living on the Skinny Branches*

Finally, a book that speaks to the lost art of appreciating others powerfully. Margo Majdi provides a penetrating insight into a basic—yet seldom mastered and rarely addressed—human need. This inspiring book is an essential read for anyone who wants to elevate his/her level of engagement with others and invite abundance and enrichment to his/her life.

**Abraham M. Turaani**
*Master Trainer & Executive Coach,*
*JADARA Training and Consulting*

In this book, Margo describes and guides us through the profound, transformational shift that one can cause in someone's life by practicing the art of acknowledgement. Margo's philosophy has transformed hundreds of thousands of lives over the years, showing that her approach works. I have personally experienced Margo's impact in impactful and significant ways, enabling many,

many individuals to create authentic and open relationships in all domains of life. This is a "must read."

**Jorge Haddock, PhD**

After reading *The Art of Acknowledgement*, I tried it with my three boys, ages 12, 10, and 7. I practiced Margo's teaching and acknowledged them and listened to them, giving them 100% of my attention. They had so much to tell me were excited to have my undivided attention. I learned so much about what they were doing in school and what is going on in their lives. From that moment on, they can't wait to share more time with me. Margo gave me the best gift and helped me realize that what I had been searching for I already possess. She gave me something immeasurable in supporting me to reconnect with my boys on a whole different level. I am truly grateful for her influence in my life.

**Auguste Davis**
*Owner of AD Private Fitness Studio, Beverly Hills*

One of our biggest needs as human beings is to feel like we matter. As we go through life, we try many avenues to fulfill that need, whether it's diet, exercise, education, work, or relationships. Many times we come up short. This book offers the solution. *The Art of Acknowledgement* is an insightful and practical guide to make people feel like they matter around us. As we advance in technology, we regress in human connection. This book puts into the foreground the value of acknowledgment and human connection.

**Chris Lee**
Transformational Coach and Trainer
Author of *Transform Your Life: 10 Principles of Abundance and Prosperity*

2

# THE ART OF
# ACKNOWLEDGEMENT

## Sacred Words that
## Elevate the Human Spirit

**Margo Majdi**

The Art of Acknowledgement

Sacred Words that Elevate the Human Spirit
Margo Majdi

Cover Photography: Rafael Najarian
Pasadena-Photography.com

Cover Make-up: Hope Zarro HopeZarroBeauty.com

Publishing Consulting: AliciaDunams.com

Printed in the United States of America

# Dedication

*This book is dedicated* to my mother, who left me when I was 12 and resides in heaven. There is not a day that has gone by that I have not acknowledged the great love, honor, and discipline she instilled in me. She taught me to look at each person as an equal, with no one lower or higher. From a young age, my mother already saw me in the highest potential.

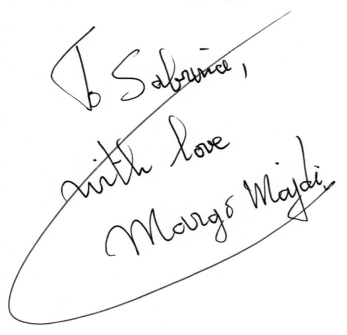

# This Book is Written

*This book is written* so that people can live each day with the purpose of acknowledgement, not just being in gratitude. But take the extra step, the effort of being thoughtful, focused out on acknowledging all that occurs in your life—coming from a higher consciousness that will make the world a better place.

# Acknowledgements

*Personally, I would like* to acknowledge all the people in my life who took the time to listen to me, love me, and support me. I acknowledge my mother and father for teaching me discipline, work ethic, and love. I acknowledge my brother, Cor, in heaven and my sister, Ria, who I always felt I can be myself with and without judgment. I acknowledge all of the teachers who stood for me in life. I acknowledge my friendships from when I was 12 years old in Holland, to today, including all of the people I adore: Ms. Vergunst, my teacher who had a huge influence on me, Cas De Geus, who was the best man to ever work for, and my dear friends, Liesbeth, Ivonne, Angela, Ronald, and Kok.

In America, I acknowledge Ms. Ruth, who gave me my first job in a beauty salon, even when I didn't have the proper license. I acknowledge all the men I used to love; you made me grow with leaps and bounds.

I acknowledge John Hanley Sr. for creating Lifespring, where I received my transformation. I acknowledge all the people who believed in me and supported me in creating Mastery in Transformational Training (M.I.T.T.), especially Lynne Shirvandehi, for being my senior and support. Lynne believed in me and was the first one to work for me, even if it was a short amount of time, while I learned the principles of running an office. I acknowledge Roger Morgan for being my right-hand person and who has stood for me and stands for me each day for the growth of Mastery in Transformational Training (M.I.T.T). For all the trainers through the years, especially Sylvia Badasci, Dr. Jorge Haddock, Krista Petty, Matt Pinto, and my two masterpieces, Chris Lee and Michael Strasner, who supported me immensely and were the catalysts and stood for the growth of M.I.T.T. in an unwavering and disciplined style. I wholeheartedly acknowledge all M.I.T.T. staff, both in the office and onsite at the trainings—we couldn't do it without your service and dedication. I acknowledge my personal assistant, Charde, for making my life easier.

Now to my beloved friends and family. I acknowledge Isabella, who chose me to be her mom. I acknowledge my godson, Chris, and my goddaughters, Kiara and Marjory. Finally, I acknowledge all my friends from all over the world; you know who you are.

I acknowledge each and every student who I have learned from and I have grown through by teaching and coaching them their self-awareness in emotional intelligence.

I acknowledge all the animals in the world (especially Skywalker and Coco Chanel, who make every day worth living).

# Table of Contents

# Foreword

*Life is filled with* ups and downs, and, if we're lucky, it's also filled with beautiful souls who support one another in good times and when those curve balls are thrown our way.

I was in the middle of a bonafide identity crisis a few years ago when simple words from someone set my sense of purpose into an entirely new and exciting trajectory, giving me breath of life again.

Without warning, I had shared with a trusted friend a recent personal journal entry that captured my secret anger, anguish, and frustration. I'd never shared such dark and negative emotions with another person, and I was terrified of what she would think of me after reading the unexpected email. Her response and its impact on me was just as unexpected, as it was filled with unconditional love, encouragement, and deep recognition. Her response brought me to tears as, for the first time in a while, I felt understood, confident, and had a sense of firm footing for a potentially new chapter of my life I'd never thought possible.

What did she do that was so powerful and life changing? She simply acknowledged me—for who I am as a woman, a friend, and a leader who impacts those around me and whose experiences get to be shared with the world through writing.

This one acknowledgement gave me the courage to start living my passion through writing and publishing, not just professionally, but from my heart, sharing my deeply personal family experiences on popular websites, such as *Elephant Journal, Medium,* and eventually *The Huffington Post* as an ongoing series that has been so well received by readers experiencing similar life circumstances that they tell me how my articles have instill joy and hope in their darkest times. What a ripple effect!

This wasn't the first time I had experienced the power of acknowledgement. I had given and received some form of acknowledgements throughout my life, but I frankly didn't have a name for it or realize its potential impact until I met Margo Majdi several years ago.

Margo started the premiere personal development training company in Los Angeles called Mastery in Transformational Training. It's emotional intelligence and personal responsibility put into action to transform an individual and their surroundings, and thousands of people have trained under Margo's care. The tools I gained from her workshops and training opportunities supported tremendous growth personally in my marriage and relationships, as well as professionally, that continues to this day. By design, Margo builds into her trainings elements of acknowledgment, the practice of communicating to another person why they matter and their impact on those around them and to the world.

If only I'd known the art of acknowledgment when I worked on Capitol Hill for a U.S. Senator and a Congressional member ... As the tenor of political rancor sharpens to the point of cutting down everyone, just imagine how civil discourse and policy outcomes could change if our elected officials and their staffs would honor one another by seeing the greatness in each other, instead of the worst. Thankfully, I now practice the art of acknowledgement in my corporate career as a senior vice president for a global brand to help make my workplace more welcoming and positive.

To acknowledge another person lets them know they are seen and valued for who they really are, and it creates an emotional connection that penetrates the souls of both people on each end of the acknowledgment, the giver and receiver. It's a type of currency whereby everyone wins, everyone's spirit is lifted, and humanity hits full potential. Just imagine our world if more people practiced the art of acknowledgement!

I can be as simple as sending an unexpected text saying, "I love you. That is all," to a friend, or asking a colleague what excites them about their job and what they'd like to do next in their career, because you see them as smart and bursting with potential. It could be sharing with someone how their idea for a new business or book penetrated you and that they're really onto something incredibly impactful. These are real examples of how I have acknowledged—and uplifted—friends, peers, and loved ones recently.

Margo's devotion to acknowledging others is prevalent in this book, which offers helpful suggestions for the most impactful words and actions to acknowledge people—and all living things—based on the roles the play in society: family, neighbors, children, educators, God, the earth, food, even pets. Indeed, everyone and everything that has the potential to fill you with life can be acknowledged. Try it, and see what happens.

Just as important, but it may not seem apparent at first, is the book's insight for how to *receive* acknowledgement. The tips for being present, to listen, trust, and believe in one's own worth are invaluable tools for all aspects of life.

Developed over decades, Margo's expertise of the art of acknowledgement makes it possible for simple words and actions to be life affirming and life changing. There's magic in the pages ahead.

I acknowledge you, the reader, for being a seeker, a force for spreading positivity, a seer of humanity's beauty, a leader.

Colleen Haggerty,
Author of the Seven Months for Seven Siblings series on *Medium* and a regular contributor to the *Huffington Post*

# Introduction

*As the founder and* president of Mastery in Transformational Training, it has been my experience that in order to get people's attention, they get to be acknowledged. Of course, that's something we already do in greetings, such as, "Oh, you look great today!", but I've found that such greetings don't produce the profound effects and relationships that stem from a personalized and sincere acknowledgement.

In my company's trainings, we have created a profound experience that is centered around acknowledgements. Now, don't confuse acknowledgements with a thank you or a statement of appreciation. They are not the same. While a thank you does, indeed, express appreciation for something a person has done (and it is fitting for that purpose), it isn't specifically *for the recipient*. That's because a thank you is also about you. After all, you wouldn't be able to thank someone if they hadn't done or said something to you and for you. A thank you requires a deed—an acknowledgement does not. An acknowledgement can be given at any time, for any reason, and sometimes for no reason at all. That is what makes acknowledgements so personal ... and so powerful. They are given freely, willingly, and without any cause, except for the fact that the person doing the acknowledging simply wants to express a sincere statement to acknowledge someone or something for their contribution to their life, community, or the world.

Because I've personally witnessed and experienced the life-changing effects of acknowledgements, I include them in my leadership trainings. I take my participants to a sacred place where acknowledgements are exchanged and experienced. The effects are both evident and immediate. And for good reason. You see, we spend our entire life, since the moment we come out of the womb, striving to feel worthy. Everyone has an unworthiness within them. Everyone. When were born, we moved away from God or our creator and immediately began seeking approval.

To be acknowledged is really feeling it and allowing it to sink in at a very deep level in the soul, which then fills that underlying assumption of a person's unworthiness. Why should we take the time to acknowledge others? The giving is in the getting, and the getting is in the giving.

The first time you are acknowledged in a profound way is memorable. For me, standing and receiving that acknowledgement was a sacred moment, so much so that it became deeply personal and embedded in my soul. The deeper the acknowledgement, even if it is a gesture, the longer it will affect and remain in the soul. In fact, acknowledgements remain in our soul and stays with us until the day we die. Thank you's do not and cannot have such a profound impact.

When you are acknowledged, you become more positive and more courageous. That is when true leadership evolves. Dr. Martin Luther King, Jr. is a perfect example. He knew his worthiness, even in a time when others didn't. Look what happened—he fought for that worthiness and for the worthiness of an entire race. That is the true power of acknowledgement and a reflection of its contribution to great leadership skills.

In sharing the power of acknowledgements and helping others appreciate and share them, I receive great satisfaction from seeing others truly believing in themselves. It has become such a significant part of my existence that it is my reason for living.

Each day is a new day. Starting today, use this book to develop the art of acknowledgement in your life. Acknowledge yourself, for you are a unique and amazing individual unlike no other. Then acknowledge others. Make a difference in their lives by acknowledging them. This includes animals and all living things—and I've included chapters on acknowledging pets and all living creatures, as well as non-tangibles, such as spirituality, governments, and cultures, to guide you through the process.

When you practice acknowledgments in a sincere way, it becomes transformational for both you and the person or thing that is being acknowledged. Of course, you will increase someone's worthiness and value, and in doing so, you'll feel great. It's true that if you want to feel great, all you have to do is make someone else feel great.

On a deeper and broader level, not only do acknowledgements impact the way we feel and make others feel, but one person at a time, they have the power to stop wars and conflicts. By appreciating and acknowledging the good qualities in a person, country, or culture, there would be nothing left to fight over. For instance, if I were to acknowledge your greatness, you would acknowledge that maybe I'm not so bad ... and you would begin to see the greatness that resides within me. Just imagine, if every person on this great earth were to acknowledge their friends and foes, it could change the world. Peace and contentment are the natural outcome from focusing out in a positive and profound way on another living thing or earthly being,

When we see the good in others and express it openly, it can only produce more goodness. It's that simple. But don't take that simplicity for granted, for acknowledgement is, indeed, an art. There is a right way, and a wrong way, to acknowledge others. In this book, I will guide you through the right way to produce the effects that will feed the soul and enrich your life and the lives of others. It requires being present, fully present in the moment, for acknowledgements are a component of communication at the most personal level. Through this book, you'll learn how to expand and enhance your communication skills to produce the most profound effects and improve your relationships. I also share experiences where acknowledgements have changed my life and the lives of so many others, from children to elders, cultures and governments, plants and animals, and those we love and work with on a daily basis.

Life and all living things are sacred. Through the sacred words and acknowledgements in this book, you have the power to elevate the human spirit and serve the world. Acknowledge it, and it will transform your life.

Margo Majdi

# Acknowledgements

*Never assume people know* what you feel and think about them, because they don't know and get to hear it from your mouth. If you ask most people, "What is your purpose of living?", typically what comes to mind is "to be happy." Well, happiness is a state of mind. The question is, "What is the purpose for living?" What makes us happy is doing the things we like to do. Then what? In the last 24 years of coaching thousands of people, I've discovered that our deepest and profound moment arrives when we are being acknowledged— acknowledged for who we are and who we have become. If you really look at people who are successful, what they all strive for, more than anything else, is acknowledgement.

There are different types of acknowledgements, and I like to define each one: eye contact, verbal, gift giving, and physical. Let's first take eye contact. Imagine being in a room full of people. Like everyone else, you are mingling among the guests. Your eyes span the room until you find that one person—your spouse or partner—and your eyes meet for several seconds. It's a personal way to acknowledge someone, letting him or her know that out of all the people around, you know they are there and they are important to you. Have you ever been in a meeting and found yourself seeking the eye of another individual when something was said? In that case, you acknowledged that person—because you are aware of their ideas, thoughts, presence, feelings, etc. In making eye contact, you let them know at that moment that they mattered to you.

When I am acknowledged, I am receiving for who I am—that another person truly sees me. Their acknowledgement is for what they see within me, not outside of me. If I do something, I make a difference with people personally and in people's lives. When I feel that I am recognized and people experience that, I feel acknowledged. By actually saying and hearing that, it makes me feel great. Just think about it. You feel great when you are acknowledged by somebody, rather than receiving a thank you, because a thank you goes back to what you did for them.

Now, people can be acknowledged for doing something good—when a child comes home with his report card and he's acknowledged for his hard work, or when they receive their diploma at graduation. What truly makes us happy is when we've achieved or accomplished something. And typically, when we give of ourselves, we've created the biggest achievement—that's when it resonates. Think about it. People fight in wars and battles. What do they do when they get home? Why do people fight wars? To give of themselves? To take the biggest risks of their lives, risking their health and their future? When some of our soldiers come back from fighting, they are acknowledged with a medal. For instance, a couple of years ago, I was watching television, and finally after 60 years, a man received his purple heart. His response was, "All my life I have been waiting for that." A week later, he passed. This man had waited his entire life for that acknowledgement of his service. Just think how his life would have been different if he had been acknowledged six decades earlier.

## Acknowledgments and Thank Yous

I believe there is a big difference between a thank you and acknowledgement. When I say, "I thank you," and you hear the "I" in it, it's really about me, not about you. Think about it—you don't have a reason to thank someone unless they have actually done something for you. "Thank you for the kind words." "Thank you for helping me today." "Thank you for bringing me such beautiful flowers." In each of these examples, the person did something and you were the benefactor of their words or actions. When you say thank you, you are acknowledging yourself and the other person at the same time. A thank you is praise, but it is not acknowledgement. However, you can acknowledge someone without them having done something special for you or giving you a reason. "Your generosity is touching and so inspiring." "I acknowledge your beautiful spirit and gentle kindness." "Wow, your smile is so radiant it lights up the room!" These examples are truly personal, and they reflect the unique characteristics and traits in a person, rather than what the person may have done or said to you. There's no right or wrong here; but there is a real difference, especially to the recipient.

Needless to say, acknowledgement needs to come from an authentic, honest place. It's not nonchalant and fake, and it should never, ever be something that's made up and untrue. If you truly acknowledge a person for who they are in life, their greatness, their power, how they've shown up, the contribution they make in the world, or simply their accomplishment, it will make them feel incredible. If you acknowledge a child for his A's and even his B's, this child will do much better. However, if you praise him/her and say you could have done better, you would invalidate everything you've just said.

Acknowledgement doesn't have to be an entire story; it's more about coming from your heart and being genuine, letting that person know how you truly feel about them.

The end result of an acknowledgement is that people feel great about themselves, because, truly, in all the things we do in life—whether you are a mother or a student, or in a relationship—we like to know that we are actually being seen for who we are and that we are being acknowledged for the difference we make in their life and in the world.

Acknowledgements have even greater benefits to the mind, body, and spirit. I have witnessed the physical power of acknowledgement in people in a room. In very sincere acknowledgements, I have witnessed people who had Rheumatoid Arthritis being able to straighten out their arthritic crippled fingers after their acknowledgements from 60 people at the same time

After sitting down and receiving hugs, she came to me and said, "Margo, look at my hands." In every meeting where I had previously witnessed her, her fingers were truly crippled. In front of my eyes, they straightened out. She also said that she didn't need any pain medication that day as a result and that she also witnessed other people receiving acknowledgement.

So being in that environment of love, where you are acknowledged and recognized for who you are and the difference you make in the world, means you actually gave of yourself. It wasn't all just about you. The changes can be astronomical. Physically, we can have a change, when it comes to pain or body language. Emotionally and spiritually, the changes can be quite significant, as well.

An acknowledgement is an act that states you recognize someone and appreciate or care about him or her. It could be a sign of respect, gratitude, sympathy, congratulations, friendliness, or spirituality. It can be deeply ingrained, as in when I acknowledge my elders, or patriotic, as when I acknowledge a country or its military. It is an act, but much more so, it conveys a strong message: you are important to me, and I recognize and appreciate you. Imagine how empowering it is to be able to touch others in such a way. Imagine the ability to make others feel valued in a world where values are often misguided. Imagine the transformation we can all make when we begin to make acknowledgements a part of our everyday lives.

How else can we acknowledge people? Handwritten notes are an excellent method. Texting is great, but there is nothing nicer than writing a note to someone, especially in this day and age with the overuse of impersonal emails and smart phones. There is something real and special about seeing someone's handwritten note, receiving it in the mail, and being able to place it somewhere and see it all the time. I was privileged to experience this. I went to visit one of my neighbors a couple of months ago, and his buddies come and shoot the breeze in his garage where he hangs out and keeps his most precious possessions, pictures of his children, fishing poles, and other manly objects. He pointed out to me that he'd kept a note from me written a while back, acknowledging his kindness as a neighbor. There it was, hanging in the middle of pictures of his family members. So, sometimes, what you might think is not significant could actually be a treasure to another person—it could change their life forever.

I had another neighbor, who I wasn't very fond of, or at least that's what I originally thought. But she was always kind enough to call me every time there was something unusual happening at my property. During my first possible opportunity to bring her flowers and acknowledge her for being such a kind neighbor and for looking out for the well-being of our neighborhood, she stood there, practically gasping for air, and said, "No one has given me flowers in the last 15 years." It changed the way I felt about her, and it was evident that my acknowledgement truly touched her and made a difference in her day, and maybe her life.

Acknowledgements don't have to be expensive—they can be free. Has a child ever given you a fistful of fresh-picked dandelions? At a young age, he or she is acknowledging you for being in their life. An acknowledgement can be as simple as surprising someone with a note that says, "I thought about you today. I hope your day is fabulous. Let's get together soon!" It didn't take much time, effort, or money, but the sentiment let the receiver know that they really do mean something to you and you want to be part of their life. Believe me, the results are quite impactful when we open our world up to those around us and let them know that they matter.

The acknowledgements we give could be in many different forms. Sometimes they are the spoken words, and sometimes they are in unspoken words. Of course, verbal acknowledgement is understood; it's expressing an acknowledgement out loud. Non-verbal can include a touch, a card, note, or photograph, or even a gift. Physical acknowledgement is quite powerful and often personal. Patting someone's hand or touching someone's arm to let them know I care is a physical acknowledgement. So is a hug. While there are varying degrees of touching, it's safe to say that physical acknowledgement is often quite personal.

I'm sure all of you could think of many other ways in which you could acknowledge somebody. I think the highest acknowledgement, however, is when someone is willing to wash somebody's feet. Just think about it—being at a family meeting or a family reunion and washing one of the elder's feet, in a ceremonious way. Initially, you may think this sounds strange. However, once you do it, you will be part of an incredible experience for both you and your family that expresses your gratitude, while honoring their contribution to your family. Take a moment to really reflect. How have we honored our elders? Or our heroes? In the Latin and Asian communities, people know how to honor their elders. I have done it with both, and the outcome was extraordinary—so big that I know that it was also extraordinary for the whole family and the highlight of all their lives together.

So, how could you create something in your family, something that could be so impactful that it could forever create an even bigger bond than ever before? Then, if you're not united as a family, what could YOU do about it?

NOW IT'S YOUR TURN

If you are in a relationship with somebody, for example, a boyfriend or husband, you could acknowledge him by saying what an incredible man he is and the difference he makes in the world. It is that simple.

"You are an incredible man, and our family looks forward to seeing you come home every night."

You are not saying <u>you</u> can't wait for him to come home, but instead, you are including the family. He needs to know that you're not the only one who he is important to—it's the family, as well, but he is the one who makes a difference.

A teacher could say to a student:

"You earned that A; you're amazing. Who knows, some day you may run the country, or have your own business, or you are going to be the best father." "Your determination and perseverance pays off when you stay committed to your studies, etc."

# Communicating

*When people are present* in the moment with their listening to hear every word you say, that is called "critical communication."

You will need to establish 100% communication so that the person speaking is aware that the other person is listening, and that when you are speaking, you are now responsible for every word that comes out of your mouth and know that the deliberate thoughts you express are what you intend them to hear.

It is critical for the other person to listen 100%.

When people are not **present**, they might miss the critical intention behind the whole conversation; for example, when people get distracted or lose their train of thought in delivering the message, the information is not fully comprehended.

- could be as a mother/father/child interaction
- could be with a teacher at school
- could be between teacher/student
- could be between employer/employee
- and the most important place, could be in court with the judge giving a judgment

Sometimes, one word being missed in the conversation (or interpreted in the way we commonly listen in our society where we think we already "heard" the information before the information is actually delivered) can make a crucial difference in what is conveyed.

A metric that can be used to support you is asking, "What did you hear me say?" and have the person repeat back what they actually heard us say. The purpose is not to make the other person feel they are inferior, because that would defeat the purpose of acknowledgements, but to know that you conceived, delivered, and executed information and they received the communication and will execute it the way it was intended. Was it totally understood the way it was meant? There are so many different interpretations we can make of a single interaction with people, friends, partners, lovers, or family. Everybody interprets the way they receive something to mean right in the moment, and that's not always the message that you were choosing to convey. Stop and think for a minute about how this could affect a relationship. Whoa, the problems that could be avoided if we could avoid confusion, misinterpretation, and misunderstanding!

It's also true that there are different forms of communication, especially with today's technology. People speak to each other in person, they communicate via telephone, send text messages, correspond via email, and use social media to interact. I am a strong advocate of face-to-face acknowledgements, but other methods are still effective. However, it's not difficult to see that acknowledging a person who is next to me is more powerful than the more impersonal text message, which, unfortunately, takes the emotion out of the acknowledgement. It's also possible that those impersonal messages can lack considerate communication and elicit the opposite effect on a person than the one that was desired. That would not be good!

Written communications can be strong acknowledgements, but one must remember that the tone behind the message can be easily misinterpreted. As much as humor is needed in life, it can be mistaken for ridicule. Even something as innocent as capitalizing a phrase or sentence can be construed as anger, when it's not intended at all. This is because written expressions lack the emotional impact of tone, facial expressions, and body language, which contribute to the message you are expressing. For those reasons, it's important to be particularly careful how you state written acknowledgements and make every effort to ensure you are conveying the right sentiment.

Also, when you communicate, as a means of validating a person while you acknowledge them for who they are or what they have done, it is important that the person is "present" to receive a validation, because if they are not present in the moment of validation or receiving, it will go right over their heads. That doesn't mean that a person must be physically on the premises and visible, though that does help—instead, that the individual is free of distractions and their mind and attention are fully present so they are fully aware.

The act of being aware is a practice. The more you become aware of when you're distracted and not in the moment, the better and faster you will be able to know when you are not. You must also become aware of when you hear a negative. For example, if you want to say something nice or positive and you hear a negative coming up, you can cancel and bring it back to the positive. Bring it back to the awareness. Bring it back to why you're there.

You always have a choice of how can you become present or how you can be aware of being present. Again, it comes back to realizing when you're not present. Ask yourself, "How do I know when I'm not present? What happens?" You might answer that you become distracted, anxious, or stressed. This is an opportunity for you to make a shift and cancel and return to the present. It's a process of acknowledging to yourself what is going on. You can take a break, pause, or simply state that you are distracted. Or you can say, "Hold on one second, I am not present. Let me just get a hold of myself. Because you are very important to me, I want to make sure I'm getting this right."

Just as in being distracted, you can often find yourself shifting from acknowledgement when you encounter negativity. Most of the time, people are used to listening to the negative, to invalidation, than truly listening and hearing validation.

People would much rather say, "Oh, you're always so mean to me or abusive to me," or be a victim of a circumstance. They would rather listen to the negative than listen to the positive, so they instantly dismiss the positive and go back to our negative. It's like 1,000 people can say how great you are, and then when one person says, "Oh, but you could have done this better," that statement becomes what you build your life on. Forever after, you now have to prove yourself, instead of receiving graciously all the positive statements, acknowledgement, and validation. People fail to receive the criticism (if you want to call it that) and look at it as constructive criticism, and embrace it.

This approach is not meant to make you feel, "Oh, I screwed up," and is not intended to garner the response, "Oh, that's your opinion." The concept is to embrace it just like all the other positives, because you know you did a great job and you have a choice to always learn or a choice to always have to defend yourself.

People often have difficulty graciously accepting a compliment or a kind gesture. Society tells you that you must be modest and humble, lest you risk being labeled as conceited, pompous, or better than others. For that reason, you downplay your importance, to yourself and to others. You need to learn how to value yourself, so you can fully value the people and things around you. That doesn't mean that you have to think you are perfect—it simply means learning to like, even love, yourself for who you are at this moment. No one is perfect. It is your uniqueness that makes you different and, yes, special. You can learn to love yourself for who you are, faults and all. For it is your faults that become your greatest learning tools. They help you see yourself in a different light—one that respects your gifts and your shortcomings. You can learn to make a mistake and be able to laugh about it, for you have brought humor into your life and the lives of others who are able to appreciate it and you. When you stop defending yourself or being critical of your shortcomings, you open yourself to love—love for yourself and love from others. Only then can you fully and openly express love for the people and things in your life.

From now on, when you, as a choice, receive a compliment, an acknowledgement, the most important thing is that you don't doubt yourself, because where there's doubt, you are constantly open in your choices to feel criticized or not. When there is no doubt, you will not interpret it as criticism, period. Let's not forget that when there is doubt, you cannot trust.

How do you go about creating trust within yourself? It's really not hard.

1. Be well-informed. In whatever you are doing—studying, making a presentation, testing, or in relationships—make sure that you are well informed, that you have studied enough to know you can make that test, receive that A, or are able to invest in the relationship at the highest level.

2. Practice your skill. If it's cooking or becoming an Olympic athlete, it all takes practice. Practice creates improvement, which increases your confidence, which creates results you are striving for.

3. In relationships, practice communication, listening, and being aware of your needs and your worthiness. In a relationship, or in the process of looking for one, if you doubt your worthiness, you will probably attract a different person than if you are clear on your worthiness, which is when you attract someone who will treasure you as a gift. When you doubt your worthiness, you will attract someone who thinks *they* are the gift. That doesn't mean that you can't look at one another as the "gift" to one another, but in this case, it relates to realizing who you will attract. Even if you attract the perfect person, doubting yourself will create a different outcome and that person will not be the perfect person—you will be coming from insecurity and will eventually push them away, because in your jealousy and insecurity, your state will not be one of bliss.

So what does a person need to do to **trust themselves** in a relationship? The person has to have confidence.

In the workplace, what do you need to do to trust yourself? You need to be informed, practice your skills, communicate, and be open to learning. You do whatever you need to do, work harder, be willing to learn about the work you do, go the extra mile, and ask for coaching.

If you are acknowledged by somebody but doubt yourself, you can't hear the acknowledgement. There's just too much doubt to believe its sincerity. I have a simple formula for everybody to use to stop doubting him or herself and to start **loving themselves—to start acknowledging themselves**. If you are not willing to love and acknowledge and appreciate yourself for who you are, nobody else will!

The simplest, and maybe one of the hardest, things to do is to write a love letter to yourself.

You probably think I've lost my mind, but I couldn't be more serious. Really, stop everything now and get a pen and paper and write a letter telling yourself just how amazing, incredible, fascinating, and worthy you are for no reason at all—simply because you exist.

You might ask, "What am I going to say?" You might feel nauseous just at the thought of it, or excited, or silly, or very, very confused. Don't put that much thought into it—it's not a contest. It's just a simple little note from yourself to yourself. Nobody is going to read it but you, so it's not like anyone is going to tell you that it's dumb or disagree with anything you say.

When you do this, I can absolutely guarantee you that you're going to be surprised at what you find out about yourself. We always think we know ourselves better than anybody knows us, but sometimes we forget to know and appreciate who we really are. That's going to stop right here.

Take the time to acknowledge the person you are, right now, just as you're standing there. It's not hard to begin.

How about starting out with a really simple acknowledgement: "Hey, you exist."

Write a list of things you acknowledge yourself for. Don't forget to be present in this moment of communication with yourself. Be aware of what you're saying, and mean it. Really mean it.

Now, look back on what you wrote. What did you learn about yourself that you didn't already know?

> *"Self-Appreciation and validation, if we can't see it in ourselves, we can't appreciate and see it in another."*
> - Margo Majdi

> *"When I look onto the world, I see no reason to be happy, which allows me to be happy for no reason."*

Make this your daily practice for one to two minutes a day. Start your day with it. You are worth it.

*Chapter 1*

# How to
# Acknowledge Children

*When I think of* home, I think of family—a parent or parents and children. Perhaps one of the most important, but often neglected, acknowledgements is that of a parent acknowledging his or her child. It could be for doing their chores, listening, coming up with a great idea, cooperating during a critical time, getting good grades, helping with a sibling, or just for being them—every child has a trait that makes him or her unique. Do they have an uncanny ability to make others laugh? Are they introspective, always giving serious thought to everything? Are they driven and responsible? Are they organized, or does their haphazardness bring spontaneity into the home? Are they caring and always trying to "take care of others?" The bonus here is that when these traits are acknowledged, the child learns to value their personality, rather than comparing it to others and finding fault with it. This can begin at a young age, and builds self-esteem and confidence.

Regardless what special talents, gifts, and traits your child may have, there is one acknowledgement that is very powerful and always appropriate. That is to acknowledge a child by telling her or him what a masterpiece he or she is: "You are a masterpiece. It is so incredible seeing you grow up and become the powerful human being that you are. I am always star struck just by looking at you. Know that everybody around you is inspired by looking at you, because of your generosity, your love, and the kindness that you are giving." Of course, you can substitute other reasons. You can also say, "You are a treasure. You are a slice of Heaven. It is an honor and a privilege to watch you waking up every morning and look into my face."

If you were a child, how good do you think that would make you feel? It is an acknowledgement that simply, but powerfully, states that you appreciate, love, and acknowledge your child for being special ... for nothing more than being who they are.

The Torch Foundation was created for teens at risk. The Torch Foundation is a non-profit that bring motivational and transformation workshops to high-risk youth. In all honesty, most teens are at risk, really. It's about creating a situation where teens receive training to learn self-development, and they become self-aware. They have a mentor for the whole month who will coach them on whatever they say they want in their life. As part of the training, they are asked to write a letter of accomplishment.

In 2006, I brought the Torch Training to China. The Torch Training is a two-day teenage training. I was invited by the Chinese government to bring this training to their country. I was interviewed by attorneys and people who work for the government. It was absolutely amazing. The person who we taught to do the training in China is like our Doctor Phil, but on Chinese television. To this day, he is still creating these trainings. I am sure he created them a little differently, as well, because their society is quite different than ours. Their main concern about their children is keeping them from falling in love. They call it "puppy love" at that age. In the United States, our greatest concern is that our teens might quit school, join a gang, do drugs, etc., but over there, it is falling in love too early in life and losing focus on their education.

At that time, parents were only allowed to have one child. Understandably in that case, the child is the most important thing they have in their life; therefore, it's vital to them that the child devotes their time to studying and becoming somebody in society. The greatest threat to that would be for the child to fall passionately in love, which we are all aware can happen during the teenage years.

At the end, we wrapped it up and I spent an evening with the mothers and fathers. I coached them on how to acknowledge their children, telling them when their child goes to bed, to whisper in their ears how incredible they are. In China, they don't have that connection, and actually, I find that most people don't have that connection with their children. I was really pleased at how well it was received. Everybody took great notes of how to acknowledge their children because they don't really hug their children in their culture. Instead, they push them to find what and how much they can do and create a vision for their life. It's not at all like acknowledging them for what they are doing at the moment. For them to even notice that children are making such great progress and wanting to study, and having the skills to study, and acknowledge their being over and over was quite transformational. It was like an awakening—a totally new concept for them. They were in tears after listening to what I said and the words they could use to say to their children. I do know they love their children deeply.

I told them to whisper beautiful things while they were lying in bed before they go to sleep, and there was not a dry eye in the whole room. They had never thought of that, and you probably haven't, either. But that is such a profound moment, to take that moment and whisper it in a child's ear. Don't say it loudly, but truly whisper, and then they can go to sleep with those words of love coming from you about who they are and, of course, who they can become in life, too.

Acknowledgement examples:

"You are Heaven-sent," or "You are a slice of Heaven," or "You are such a gift to this world and our family." "You are an honorable son," or "You are an honorable daughter." "You amaze me every day. When I see you walking through the door, my heart just gets butterflies. You are like a butterfly because we are watching you transform into this beautiful person that you are."

It was really profound for them, and something everyone can find insightful. Sometimes the simplest thing, just telling he/she how incredible he/she is, not just how beautiful he/she is, because he/she probably hears that—though some children sadly don't hear that from their mother or father ever

This acknowledgement speaks to the child's soul. So whatever your child is doing, whether it's sports, academics, ballet, or chores at the home, acknowledge them for what they did, not for what they didn't do or could have done better. The moment you say, "You could have done better," or even if you say, "We have an A, but can you get an A+," you invalidate them right there on the spot. Acknowledge them for what is, not what isn't. It's a different interaction, but make that particular moment so profound that it will stay in their soul and their spirit.

That awareness enticed the Chinese group of coaches and trainers to come to the U.S. a couple of years later. Nineteen of them came to America, and I had them all stay over at my house. There were 13 girls and 3 boys, and 3 supervisors. The gentleman who did the training is a psychologist in China, like Dr. Phil on TV, and he came, as well.

One young lady, who was 13 years old at the time, came to me one morning and after I hugged her, she asked, "Would you be my mother?" I was taken aback and shocked. I couldn't tell her "no." How cruel would that be? Besides, I didn't want to. Her request really made me feel honored. So I said, "Yes," and then I said, "So, why do you ask me? Don't you have your mother? Because one thing I don't like to do is to take the place of someone's mother, because everybody has a mother, and we get to honor our mother." She told me no, her mother had passed away a year before.

I could so relate to that because my mom had passed away at exactly her age. Up to this day, I still feel that pain. So for her to ask me to be her mom, and letting me step into just a little bit of that role, was quite an honor for me. It still is. She is now 19 years old, lives in America, and is going to college here. I know she will study and become somebody big in her life. She is the daughter in my life. I could not have done a better job than her mother did because she raised an amazing human being. I am so proud of her and fortunate that she calls me her mom.

When was the last time you acknowledged your children?

| Sacred Words to Use: | |
|---|---|
| • Respect | • Love |
| • Like | • Admiration |
| • Pride | • Honor |
| • Incredible | • Joy |
| • Pleased | • Grateful |
| • Contribution | • Togetherness |

Examples of an acknowledgement to a child:

"Every time I open the door, I witness sunshine, even when it is a cloudy day. Look at the impact you make and will make on the world."

"How beautiful is it to look in your loving eyes."

## Chapter 2

## How to Acknowledge
## School and Education

*An education is important,* and it is something that holds real value. Those who educate us provide us with a lifetime gift, and too often, we overlook the importance of expressing our appreciation for the contribution they are making in our lives. Whether one is completing high school, post-graduate school, returning after many years to pursue a degree, or taking a workshop or classes for self-improvement or professional development, there is much to appreciate. One is a teacher who truly impacts our lives, motivates, inspires, or finds a way to express a concept so it is easy to understand. Others include a counselor who truly listens, or a cafeteria worker who never fails to smile and spread cheer. There are bus drivers or security guards who go out of their way to ensure safety and orderliness, and office personnel who take the time to learn our names and go out of their way to help. We can acknowledge a classmate who shares notes or supplies or offers assistance, and coaches and assistants who provide us with extracurricular activities.

Acknowledge them by sending them a message, note, card, or letter. Tell them that they made a difference in your life and your ability to learn. Knowing that they made a difference in your life and future can be very fulfilling, and it will give them the motivation to instill their knowledge, care, and talents upon other students in the days and years to come.

---

**Sacred Words to Use:**

*I acknowledge you for the_____ in my child's life:*

- Growth
- Devotion
- Commitment
- Impact
- Security
- Knowledge
- Understanding
- Dedication
- Service
- Guidance
- Wisdom
- Trust

---

Sacred Acknowledgements:

- I acknowledge you for your commitment to humanity, society, the love and discipline you instill in our future leaders, your passion and compassion.

- You never give up on anyone in your classroom.

- The look in your eyes says how much they mean to you when you speak about them.

- They grow each day in knowledge because of your determination.

# Chapter 3

## How to Acknowledgement
## Your Spouse or Partner

*In the beginning of* every relationship, there is joy in learning every little thing about an individual. You love their intricacies, their past, their dreams, their talents, their hobbies and interests, their physical features, and their personalities. Over time, however, you can fall into a routine. You know each other too well, take each other for granted, and sometimes, the things you once loved become annoying. The coffee that was made and poured before you got out of bed becomes an expectation, rather than a very appreciated loving act. Intimate relationships lose their intimacy and passion when they are not acknowledged. They fall into a routine and daily lives take over, replacing the special aspects of a spouse, who might no longer feel valued. How much would that relationship strengthen if you acknowledged their role and impact on your life?

One of the most powerful acknowledgements I've ever heard took my breath away, this person said to his partner, "You are the center of my thoughts." Whoa, that's a good one to use! Another one was, "I leave the door open to my dreams so only you can keep me company."

If your partner or spouse acknowledged you in such a way, imagine how very special it would make you feel.

Of course, acknowledging your spouse by seeing what he or she did for you, and does for you all the time, is important. But it's the love and their presence in your life that is most significant; let them know that the love they bestow upon you is worth living for each day.

That's what relationships and marriages are about—it's what we strive and live for. It's one thing to bring home more and more money, but it's so important to also hear the words. I had an experience once where a lady said, "You know, my husband never says he loves me." I responded, "Wait a minute, didn't he buy you five cars and you live in a mansion and have like 19 different fur coats?" She answered, "Yeah, but he never says that he loves me."

Isn't it interesting that she needed to be recognized for the love she gives, instead of giving and receiving all those gifts? To her, what was missing in her life were words. The words you get to hear from the other person, to acknowledge that person, by saying, "You are the best mother to our children," or "We are so fortunate that you chose to be in our life," can be worth more than anything in the world. Make the acknowledgement constantly about that person, even if what they did was for you. Always make it about that person, not what they did or how you felt.

It is the sacred words that are an acknowledgement, not a fur coat, diamond ring, or a car. People keep wanting to make more and more money; they think the money and what they are going to buy with it is important. In the end, it's the people. For instance, look at rich people and those times when their housekeepers are gone and they can actually tend to the fireplace or cook for themselves. That's when they feel like they have the best evening at home with their wife or spouse.

It is not only the words; of course, there are actions. "Actions speak louder than words" – the actions have got to match the sacred words that are spoken.

I'm not refuting that gifts are nice. Of course, it is beautiful to have a gift bestowed upon you; but if it is a gift given to make up for something, it takes on the form of a manipulation. If it is a gift because you wanted it for a long time and somebody took an extra job to buy it or invested in the extra time to find it for you. That makes all the difference. Even if it's something hand-made and the person actually took the time to create or carve something, or they wrote a poem for you—it is something special that speaks about you, not about his/her ego.

It's also up to you how to receive that, to really take it in. If you think you're not worthy of anything, you're not going to cherish it, either; but if you know that you are worthy of it, then you will cherish it.

The giving has got to come from an authentic place, not from manipulation. The reason for this is that a lot of times the underlying purpose of giving is to be noticed. If you give somebody a big car, it may be because you want to be noticed for the extravagance of the gift you gave. Or maybe you were finally able to buy the car, but instead of you having the car, you'll acknowledge your spouse in that she or he gets to have that car. Acknowledgement is about where it comes from. If you start acknowledging people because you know it sounds good, that's wrong. It's got to be authentic. It's got to come from a place in your heart to the other person's heart.

It's about love, love, love, love. The word love is used in such an easy and free way. Sometimes, it's almost like saying hello to somebody. I don't think we should make the word so insignificant by using it so much that it doesn't really have any meaning or love behind it. Love is an incredibly big word. So is compassion. To me, compassion is much more important than love, because compassion can be felt even if you don't love someone.

In my trainings, we have a ceremonial acknowledgement for all the people who are graduating. I am going to share a time where I witnessed a gentleman who was acknowledging his wife (I see that frequently) and the incredible words he spoke to her of how she is his inspiration every day.

He acknowledged her for being his inspiration and for taking on her life in such a way that their marriage is in such an incredible position of love, honor, compassion, and passion for one another. It truly took my breath and everybody else's breath away. He acknowledged her for the astonishing results that she creates in her life by saving so many people in the world (she is a doctor). He stated that every day waking up next to her was a privilege. At the end of the acknowledgement, he bowed and kissed her feet. Needless to say, there wasn't a dry eye in the room, because of the emotion that it brought forward in all of us, including myself. That's what everybody would like to have in their relationship.

It's not that you should do it for the hell of doing it—it's got to have a whole emotional journey that you both went through to get to that point. That's how impactful it is to have that experience in a moment of time. I guarantee it will never leave her experience, and I know the emotion and the impact it had will last till the day she dies. She was truly honored—according to the Bible, the biggest honor you can bestow on somebody is to acknowledge them and kiss their feet, or wash their feet.

In the morning when she wakes up, a man could say to his wife in very few words, "You're a goddess." Just three words: You're a goddess. I guarantee, during the whole day and maybe for the rest of her life, she will remember those three words. Because I'm sure she has heard, "I love you" often, but the 'I' is in the way. 'You're a goddess' lands in a different way.

Types of acknowledgements: Verbal, written. Flowers, cards, notes. Special dinner. Pack a lunch. Buy a gift. Back rubs. Running fingers through hair. Reaching out and touching a hand. Non-verbal interaction, connecting with each other's eyes. A special intimate night. Breakfast in bed. Sharing memories. Making a sacrifice for each other. Compromise. A surprise note of encouragement. An unexpected phone call in the middle of the day. An impromptu romantic date.

Other acknowledgements could be holding hands for a half hour a day, without saying a word. No matter what, even if one is not pleased with their partner, it's important to be committed to breaking through whatever it is, but still being able to feel the acknowledgment. Even when there is anger, with acknowledgments, any relationship can survive. It is magical, but it does require 100 percent commitment to the relationship. It's simple, but the acknowledgment that you care is the greatest symbol and expression of love.

*I cherish you.*

---

**Sacred Words to Use:**

- Heart
- Soul
- Intimacy
- Special
- Desire
- God / Goddess
- Trust
- Secure/Security

- Love
- Cherish
- Honor
- Joy
- Fulfilling
- Togetherness
- Honesty
- Compassion

---

Sacred Acknowledgements:

- Heart: Your heart is as beautiful as you are.

- Soul: Your soul is so giving and good. I know of no one with such a pure and sincere soul.

- Love: You are love. It radiates around you.

- Intimacy: The intimacy you bring to relationships is so deep and close.

- Special: You make every day a special and exciting one

- Desire: My deepest desire is to make you happy— you mean that much to me.

- Fulfilling: The love you share is so fulfilling. I couldn't ask for more.

- Trust: Trust is one of your most incredible qualities. It truly is a symbol of the confidence we have in each other.

- Secure: There is such a secure feeling when you come home. You make our family feel whole.

- Honesty: Your honesty is commendable.

- Compassion: It is the compassion you show toward me every day that makes you so incredibly special.

- Each day, you inspire me to work harder. You are the most confident man for a family that everyone looks up to you. Your words are impactful. Your charm is enduring. You are a king. You are royalty. Everybody takes notice when you walk into a room. You are a stand for our families. Your love is breathtaking. Your compassion and generosity are so impactful. Nobody comes close to your beauty. You are golden.

## Chapter 4

# How to Acknowledge
# Family at Family Events

*Life gets in the way,* and it's easy for people to stray from their families, especially those who are not considered immediate family. Even parents, grandparents, aunts, uncles, cousins, and relatives may become more distant parts of your life—not because you want them to be, but because you get caught up in the demands and responsibilities—the busyness—of life. Yet, when you see each other again after some time, you wish we could do it more often. Often, the happiness of the occasion is surprising. It's not only a celebration of an event, but also of the people.

Weddings are a great example, but so are funerals. Saying hello and saying goodbye are both powerful, and the ways that you say those things have a huge impact on yourself and the people around you.

How can families acknowledge each other during weeknight suppers, or birthday dinners? A weekday supper can be everyone sitting around the table at the same time and having every person contribute to the conversation by telling what they did that day. The important part is to acknowledge what they said and make them feel like a valued member of the family unit.

Listen and let them know that their life today matters to you. When it's your immediate family at the dinner table, acknowledging all for being the family that you are and what an honor and privilege it is to be a part of this family is appropriate. Acknowledge them for sitting at the table because these days that doesn't happen too often. Acknowledge that, as a family, you do this consistently and are being taught the rituals of keeping the family dinner going. For a parent to acknowledge that is to always be present in what's going on in the family.

A simple, but effective, acknowledgement is for everybody to share what they did during the week, even if it's something small. How beautiful it is when a child, whether they are two or seventeen years old, gets to share what they did! What a cool thing that would be, even if it's on Sunday morning for breakfast and it is your ritual, or if it's a Saturday or Sunday night dinner. Make it a ritual that your family sits at the dinner table and shares what they learned during the week. Use it as an opportunity to truly acknowledge that person for who they are, not just being grateful for them. Acknowledge who they are and what they did. For example:

"You are such a great sister! What you did was just amazing. You are so supportive, helpful, and incredible! "

The family ritual allows everyone to know what the other did during the week; then, one at a time, acknowledge the person for that. That is a great process because everybody might say something different that happened that week, but it's so beautiful also that the others are present and listening to them. By itself, that is already the acknowledgment. Actually listening to the other human being is the acknowledgement. It's so important to actually hear what they say, instead of thinking they said something else. Truly listening to every word they're saying is a strong acknowledgement.

Listening is an acknowledgment. That is why I suggest starting by asking how their week was. 'What did you learn this week? What did you do this week?' Think about it. If everybody really listens to how their week was and then they are acknowledged later, what a great ritual it would be. Listen, truly listen, as they talk; then before the meal is over, say, "I acknowledge you for how you listen to me. I acknowledge you for listening." And to the little two year old, "I acknowledge you for growing up to be so smart." Of course, always acknowledge the person who made the meal and acknowledge the person who supported him/her in making the meal. It becomes a habit. Once you practice it at home, it becomes automatic. If you are learning this at home at a young age, just think how much of an impact it will have if you will be doing it for the rest of your life.

This family acknowledgement also applies to extended family, larger family events, get togethers, wedding, birthdays, and other celebrations. Especially when sitting down together is infrequent, it's an opportunity to make a powerful impact on the lives of the people in your family and life.

We applied this meal setting in the Torch Training we do for children. On Saturday night after the training, they are trust-walked and blindfolded while walking to the table. These are kids at risk; and they are being trust-walked, which is quite impressive in itself. We make it something quite beautiful and extraordinary. They have a special dinner setting, and we acknowledge them just by the dinner setting alone. There are rose petals, candles on the table, and beautiful crystal and porcelain plates. Believe it or not, some kids have never seen that.

When they open their eyes, they are taken away by the specialness and beauty and say, "Ahhh." Just the love of that acknowledgement is moving. It's not about the food; it's about the ritual and that they are being acknowledged because they're special.

Graduations are another milestone, one that is usually triumphed and congratulated. How can it be more meaningful? How can one acknowledge the person—and not just the diploma? These are just a few of the types of family events that can be acknowledged, in a meaningful and personal way.

If I had a *flower*
for every time you made me
smile and laugh
I'd have a garden to walk in
*forever*

| Sacred Words to Use: | |
| --- | --- |
| • Congratulations | • Prayer |
| • Treasure | • Pride |
| • Admire | • Inspiration |
| • Respect | • Joy |
| • Family | • Grateful |
| • Contribution | • Togetherness |

Sacred Acknowledgments:

- Congratulations! Great job!

- Prayer (often said at meals, weddings, etc.)

- You are the pride of our family,

- Your hard work and determination is noted and admired!

- Your journey is amazing and so successful!

- The beauty of your love is an inspiration.

- Our time together is special and a treasure.

- If there is a poet in the family, have them share one poem, song, or prayer. It is a privilege and honor to have you in our family.

# Chapter 5

# How to
# Acknowledge Ceremonies

*Acknowledgement as ceremony is* remarkable and memorable. It places a symbolic honor and spirituality to an acknowledgment. A perfect example is the washing of one's feet.

Washing one's feet was practiced in the Bible. Jesus washed people's feet, so I do not think there is a greater honor that you can bestow upon others than washing their feet. More so than your immediate family, it is a sign of honor and respect for elders. It might be Christmas, Thanksgiving, or a wedding anniversary for your grandparents or great grandparents. How beautiful it would be if, once everybody acknowledges the family, you ask them to close their eyes, put them in the middle of the room, take off their socks and shoes and play some beautiful music. Then have the smallest child, or a teenager, bring water to their feet. When they open their eyes, the family will be on their knees, surrounding them. In silence, they wash their feet in a bucket or tub of water with rose petals drifting in it. Look them in the eyes and have them experience this without any words.

I have seen this done many times in different settings. I have seen people who practically faint, so watch for signs of that and make sure that there is water for them to drink because it will take their breath away. It is that profound. On the other hand, if it's not done in the right moment, they might laugh so be aware that you create the right atmosphere for this type of meaningful ceremony.

The Pope washed the feet of twelve prisoners, including a female. Yes, change is occurring everywhere.

Another celebratory acknowledgement is bowing in honor, which is expected in many countries and cultures, but is not a common practice in the United States.

Again, there are different cultures. In the Asian countries, they bow. When I was there and we gave teenagers certificates for completing the Torch Training, they all bowed when they received their certificate. It was so beautiful.

People bow when service members come back from war. In Asian countries, bowing is such a common practice that they bow when they give your credit card back to you at the hotel. In the United States, bowing is such a rarity that it can be construed as mockery, though we will sincerely bow to someone if we feel they're amazing.

Think about it—our servicemen fight for all of us, we should bow for them each time we see them in uniform. Of course, servicemen salute one another, and that's also an acknowledgement. I remember being acknowledged many times, but the times that somebody would stand before me and acknowledge and salute me took my breath away and brought me to tears.

Bowing is about the relationship you have with others. It's honoring your elders, their past, their service, their sacrifices, contributions, nationality, culture, and traditions. Naturally, there are elders who have served in the service. Some may have received a medal for their service or heroic acts. Of course, they did not serve for the medal, but they received one as an acknowledgment. How can you honor our servicemen and women coming back, and more so, how can you acknowledge them when they are in the 60s, 70s, or 80s? How can you take special time to honor them and let them know that they have never been forgotten?

Of course, there are special days of honor for such instances, such as Veteran's Day. That day is marked to recognize those who have served. How can you do that for all of your elders? How can you honor and acknowledge them? If a special day can be created for everybody, such as the 4th of July or Independence Day, why couldn't one be created in families? Make it a special day that every family could create, designating one day for elders or the family—a day dedicated to honor and celebrate them.

---

### Sacred Words to Use:

- Respect
- Honor
- Esteem
- Homage
- Tradition
- Culture
- Consideration
- Value
- Revere
- Praise
- Humble
- Ritual

Sacred Acknowledgements:

- I acknowledge and respect you for your devotion and contribution to the family.

- I appreciate your consideration for all of the members of our family.

- I honor and value your presence. You are an honorable son and family member.

- You are of high esteem. You are such a worthwhile member of our family. We look up to you.

- Your homage and history are revered by our family.

- We pay homage to your rich background and the many contributions you've made that have enriched our family and its history.

- Your background and life are amazing and deserving of appreciation and praise.

- Our family's traditions and cultures have been enhanced by you and your background.

- This ritual is in honor of the love you have given and in appreciation for the gifts you've shared.

- Your life experiences are both amazing and humbling

- What an amazing history you have! Your culture is fascinating!

## Chapter 6

# How to Acknowledge
# God, Universe, and Higher Power

*Most people pray to* God because they want to get something. Instead, why not take a moment every day to exactly acknowledge God for all the beauty in everything He bestows and the grace He bestows upon you?

Yes, when you pray to God or a higher power, you are acknowledging His existence. But that is not the form of acknowledgement that we are referring to. It is not that you should pray to God, "Now can you give me a son or a daughter," or asking for whatever your desire is, "Find me a new job." Instead, it's the power of truly taking time to acknowledge God for the beauty and the privileges He has bestowed upon you to live this life.

You can acknowledge God by going to church, by sharing your knowledge and love for God with others so that other people know that God exists and God inspires. In that way, you get to inspire them also and bring people to God and to the church. To me, that is also acknowledging God. You don't necessarily have to visit a church; there are also chapels, hospitals, and even other institutions that offer places of worship.

Reading a Bible or other spiritual work is a way to acknowledge God or religion. Attending study groups or prayer circles is a way to increase and expand your knowledge, share it with others, and instill it in your daily life. Volunteering for a church event or cause is also appreciated and welcome.

Of course, one of the greatest acknowledgements you can give God is to be the example of what God does in your life. That is a gift that speaks for itself. Emulating God or a higher power, religion, or spirituality in your life and instilling their beliefs as you live from day to day, is the highest compliment and testament to the impact they have on you and their importance in your existence.

Occasions: often we turn to a higher being during ceremonies: Easter, Christmas, etc., weddings, funerals.

What is it that you are acknowledging God, Jehovah, Allah, etc., for?

| Sacred Words to Use: | |
| --- | --- |
| • Grace | • Universe |
| • Meekness | • Humble |
| • Peace | • Glory |
| • Acceptance | • Guidance |
| • Strength | • Knowing |
| • Faith/Faithful | • Holy/Holiness |
| • Spiritual | |

Sacred Acknowledgements:

- Your divine grace is profound and everlasting.

- The universe is only possible because of your magnificent presence and vision.

- The forgiveness you bestow inspires meekness.

- Your holy presence is cause for humble admiration.

- The world acknowledges the peace in your teachings.

- Oh, the magnificence of your glory!

- There is no greater acceptance than that which is bestowed by you.

- The guidance you grant upon those who follow is the path to righteousness.

- Your strength is infallible and worthy of praise.

- You are knowing of all and everything. That knowing brings peace and acceptance to all.

- Your faithful service inspires others to be faithful servants.

- Your presence is a spiritual blessing to the universe that is acknowledged and embraced.

## Chapter 7

# How to Acknowledge
# the Earth

*I heard a story*, that has scientific backing, that shows that we are meant to connect with the earth on a very basic level. People who have high blood pressure have been encouraged to use the practice of "grounding." In grounding, one is barefoot and outdoors. They stand on the grass where their feet come into direct contact with the earth and can see immediate benefits as their blood pressure drops – it reminds us that we are connected on a deeper level, and our survival stems from and depends on the earth.

Too often, today, people live indoors—they live in apartments and high-rises, with comforts such as air conditioning, heat, electricity, electronics, etc., that make their lives easier. They travel in vehicles, trains, buses, planes, and get their food from concrete retail stores. Being outdoors is no longer a big part of their lives. People don't smell the earth and feel the rain and the wind. They forget that their food sources come from the earth and that energy comes from the sun.

Other cultures respect the earth—without taking advantage of what it provides. They bless it, praise it, value it, and respect the resources and their role as their life source. The Indians have a profound connection with and respect for our environment. They stress preservation and believe man is second to Mother Earth—the source of all life and energy. I once met an incredible and amazing Indian man. He was a healer and told me that he was taught since he was three years old to listen to the earth because the earth has many secrets to tell us. I think that is so true.

You should acknowledge the earth for what it does for you because without the earth, you wouldn't be living. The earth provides us with the circle of life, from grass and vegetation, to crops and vegetables that feed people and animals, as well as our life source, which is water. Yet, people never really take time to acknowledge the earth. How incredible it would be if everyone started acknowledging Mother Earth for all the gifts that she gives daily! I know it all comes from God, but it is so important to become conscious of what the earth does for us.

When people don't acknowledge the earth, and for instance, cut all the trees down in the forest, I think the earth gives them pay back for violating it. People are not conscious of the effects of their actions, even from waste, with plastics and Styrofoam that pollute our land and shores. When those things are put into the earth, they poison the earth, and there will be consequences.

The earth is a living thing. Therefore, I believe it responds generously when it is appreciated and acknowledged for its role as a supporter of life, food, water, and heat. As long as you honor any living thing, it will respond to you. It is the law of cause and effect.

Acknowledgements are about opening and enforcing relationships, with people, with things, with spirituality, and with the earth.

Acknowledgements accomplish five things:

Number one, it gets their attention.

Number two, it opens the person or thing to receive.

Number three, acknowledgment opens them up to hear what you have to say.

Number four, it opens them up to give.

Number, five, it gives them the opportunity to give back, or pay it forward.

The earth is as receptive to these five causes and effects as people are. Everyone and everything is affected by outside factors. When you acknowledge that which is important to you, your relationship with it is strengthened. As a result, it hears you and you now have its attention. In return, it is open to giving more of the things you value and acknowledge.

**Sacred Words to Use:**

- Sustenance
- Preservation
- Rich
- Harvest
- Tranquility
- Nourishment

- Blessing
- Sacred
- Plentiful
- Abundance
- Beauty
- Shelter

Sacred Acknowledgements:

- You are the source of all sustenance, for animals, plants, people, and all forms of life.

- The benefits of the earth are a blessing to those who respect it

- The richness and nourishment of soil, rock, and water are the source of life's preservation

- This ground is sacred and the creation of a higher being. As such, it is to be treated with regard for its contributions.

- The earth is richer than money. It is the source of all richness and life.

- Oh, how plentiful is the earth! It provides shelter and housing and is the source of magnificence, beauty, and life.

- I acknowledge the earth's harvest as the sustenance for all life and living things.

- What abundance the earth brings as it feeds and provides shelter, water, clothing, and beauty to all creatures.

- The peaceful tranquility of the earth's many beauties is to be awed by all.

- The plants, flowers, mountains, oceans, and plains are a thing of beauty and a sight to behold.

- The earth is the sole source of all nourishment, for humans, animals, plants, wildlife, and creatures big and small.

- There is no shelter that is not reaped from the earth. Its protection is vital to all life.

# Chapter 8

# How to Acknowledge
# Food, Plants, and Flowers

*The world is robust* with life, and much of what the earth brings provides you with sustenance. The water gently washes and feeds soil and plants, producing a harvest of different nutrients, flavors, vegetables, fruits, and herbs – for food, health, and medicine. There is a delicate balance, based on geographic locations, where the richness of the environment provides harvests that thrive in a particular climate.

Acknowledging food and its source, as well as those who plant, nurture, cultivate, and harvest it is one way to acknowledge food and our dependency on it. Acknowledge those who pack it, prepare it, and distribute it, as well. It is vital to your health and survival. This includes farmers, truck drivers, produce workers, butchers, fishermen, chefs, cooks, and servers.

Food is also a staple in celebrations, family time, traditions, etc. Acknowledge the food that is served for such gatherings and celebrations and the contribution it makes to the gathering and the family. Food is and has always been an integral element in cultural celebrations.

## Sacred Words to Use:

- Sustenance
- Bounty
- Cultivate
- Delicious
- Nutrition
- Enrichment
- Feast
- Harvest
- Nourish
- Hearty
- Abundance
- Senses

Sacred Acknowledgements:

- Do not let us forget the sustenance of seeds, roots, plants, flowers, and their fruits and their abundant supply.

- Every meal that is prepared is a feast to behold.

- There is no greater bounty than that which is prepared first by the soil.

- Farmers are to be commended for their knowledge and effort in harvesting the earth's riches.

- Those who cultivate the earth give it new birth and life.

- I acknowledge the farmers, fishermen, truck drivers, grocers, and cooks for the nourishment they provide on a daily basis.

- The meal you have set before me is delicious.

- There is nothing heartier than the nourishment provided by the earth.

- Please accept my humble and grateful acknowledgment of the nutrition you bring to the world through your work and dedication.

- There is magnificent beauty in the flowers that grace the landscape for all to see.

- What abundance you have brought to others through your chosen profession!

- The earth's bounty that you have enriched and harvested is a delight to the senses!

## Chapter 9

# How to Acknowledge
# Living Things

*Every living thing has* a purpose. People all have a purpose—for themselves, to each other, and to the universe. All creatures, big or small, have a purpose. Insects, too, have a purpose and their lives and contribution to the balance of our world cannot and should not be overlooked.

Right now, the world is suffering from a lack of bees. Bee colonies have decreased significantly, and unfortunately, most people are not aware that bees are vital to our existence. Every single thing that grows, including food, plants, flowers, etc., depends on bees for pollination. Without pollination, they will die. Without plants, people and animals will fail to thrive and even exist. Such is the case with all living creatures—they play a role in the balance of our universe. From keeping overpopulation of one species in check to providing sustenance to another species, there is a circle of life that revolves around all living creatures.

Everything adds beauty, from a caterpillar that transforms to a gentle, beautiful butterfly, to a bird, that lends its song to life's melody.

Two of all living things of flesh were brought to the ark to ensure their preservation so that future generations would benefit from their existence and contribution to the planet.

Here are two quotes that reinforce this:

*This world is indeed a living being endowed with a soul and intelligence ... a single visible living entity containing all other living entities, which by their nature are all related.*
– Plato

*According to Buddhism, the life of all beings – human, animal or otherwise – is precious, and all have the same right to happiness. It is certain that birds, wild animals – all the creatures inhabiting our planet – are our companions. They are a part of our world, we share it with them.*
– The 14th Dalai Lama'

My animals are some of my most important living things. I acknowledge my animals every day—they love to hear acknowledgements, believe it or not. They love it when you say thank you to them or acknowledge them. I always acknowledge my dog, stating how fortunate we are to have him. It's about me, too—that I have this dog and that he chose me. By acknowledging my dogs, I value them and the special place they hold in my life.

With animals, acknowledgement rituals might take the form of a physical touch, massage, or speaking to them in a soothing and loving manner. I know I have their attention because they reciprocate; they know when they're being acknowledged and express it by wagging their tails.

Acknowledging dogs or animals is giving them their own place in the house where they feel comfort and security, taking care of them, cleaning them, and giving them attention. It's loving them and talking to them. Talk to them and let them know how much you appreciate them. Do not reserve this solely for dogs or cats, but every living animal, including a cow, a horse, a bird, or a squirrel (to name a few). Acknowledge them and let them know how much you appreciate them. They should know that.

Again, it is about cause and effect. When you acknowledge animals, they respond. In turn, they are more receptive to you and what you teach, say, and offer, and they give more back to you, in the form of companionship, loyalty, work, etc.

| **Sacred Words to Use:** | |
|---|---|
| • Value | • Contribution |
| • Life | • Sustenance |
| • Survival | • Mercies |
| • Harmony | • Togetherness |
| • Caring | • Respect |
| • Joy | • Companionship |
| • Comfort | • Loyalty |

Sacred Acknowledgements:

- There is value in your contribution to my life.

- Rescues and animal protection agencies provide an invaluable contribution to the safety and health of the animals that bless the earth.

- The existence of all creatures, large and small, is an amazing part of the circle of life.

- I acknowledge cattle, pigs, lambs, and chickens for the sustenance they provide to human beings.

- The contribution animals make by providing nourishment is a source of survival for all creatures.

- There are tender mercies for all life; I acknowledge their presence and role in our existence.

- All living creatures are worthy of our humble acknowledgement.

- How impressive it is that we can live in harmony with the earth's creatures!

- I acknowledge you, dear pet, for the comfort of our togetherness and acceptance.

- There is no greater deed than caring for a defenseless animal and those that have been neglected or abused.

- I acknowledge and respect rescuers and animal protection organizations, such as PETA, ASPCA, Friends of Animals, Best Friends Animal Society, for their unselfish devotion and care to animals in need.

- Dear Pet, your love is evident and returned freely.

- A beloved pet is one of life's joys that should not be taken for granted. I acknowledge and hold it dear.

- Your companionship is a cherished gift that is invaluable.

- There is no greater loyalty than that of an animal and its unselfish devotion.

*Chapter 10*

# How to Acknowledge
# Country, Government, and Freedom

*Patriotism can be deeply* seeded and reinforced from the time of our youth; it can grow gradually or suddenly, given circumstances and incidents, such as 9/11. Governments protect and provide for the safety and liberties of its citizens, while also creating laws that ensure freedom and lawfulness.

Freedom is something that is easy to take advantage of—especially for those who have not experienced any restrictions on their freedoms. Regardless, it shouldn't be taken for granted—freedom is not free and came about due to great sacrifices.

While one may not always agree with politics, motives, laws, etc., most people have a loyalty toward their country and the opportunities and lifestyles it provides. These should not be taken for granted.

There are many ways to acknowledge country, government, freedom.

Supporting those who serve is one—how powerful an acknowledgement it is to send a note and package to someone who is thousands of miles away from their home and family, serving their country. Let them know their efforts have not gone unnoticed and are appreciated—that you care about them and the job that they are doing. You respect their sacrifices, their dedication, loyalty, and patriotism.

Other acknowledgements could be as simple as singing the country's anthem, placing a hand over the heart, removing one's hat, saluting, paying tribute by attending events and rallies, or saying the Pledge of Allegiance.

When people talk about government, it is often opinionated and negative. The good things are rarely said. What if we could acknowledge our government, instead of criticizing it all of the time? Just think about the energy, the positive energy we would put out if we all started acknowledging our government. I'm from Holland, and we have a saying, 'Unity creates power,' 'Eenheid maakt macht.'

Unity creates power. The more unified the message, the stronger it is. This is true whether the message is positive or negative. One of the reasons people believe that our country is moving backward and not progressing in a positive manner is that there are so many who express negative opinions about our country. Once we shift our energy and acknowledge the freedom and the opportunity we still have in this country, we can create a positive impact on our country and government.

Here is one way to acknowledge government. When exposed to the negativity, right away make an observation and speak up. Ask, "So what is it that you're going to do for your country?" I think John Kennedy said that so well, which is why most people loved John Kennedy—he brought something out in them. He listened, but he also expressed to the people that everything isn't the government's responsibility—it's up to the people, as well. When you speak up, you can make a difference.

| **Sacred Words to Use:** | |
| --- | --- |
| • Allegiance | • Loyalty |
| • Tribute | • Admiration |
| • Respect | • Honor |
| • Patriotism | • Protection |
| • Homage | • Integrity |
| • Sacrifice | • Bravery |

Sacred Acknowledgements:

- I acknowledge soldiers for their undivided allegiance to our country and its principles.

- The loyalty in which public servants do their job is commendable.

- Your service is held in highest regard and deserving of the highest tribute.

- As a fireman (policeman, paramedic, etc.), you have served with honor and grace.

- All police and protectors of the law have earned respect for the amazing way they carry out their duties under pressure and without regard for their own safety.

- Your devotion and desire to care for and treat those in need is a thing of admiration.

- I acknowledge all branches of the military and veterans for the patriotism they displayed in answering the call for service and carrying out their duties.

- The protection you have provided to those in need has not gone unnoticed.

- Paying homage to those who sacrifice for our country is the right thing to do every day.

- The integrity you displayed is an example for all.

## Chapter 11

# How to Acknowledge
# Other Nations

*Instead of throwing bombs* and finding fault in differences, educating oneself about other countries, their politics, their causes, their beliefs, traditions, and struggles can create a new and profound understanding and appreciation for each other. Lives would be saved, resources spared, anger and animosity erased. Friendships could develop where there once was hate, compassion where there once was ignorance, and commendation instead of condemnation. This could also build a newfound respect for other beliefs, traditions, cultures, and values.

There are wars being fought all over the world. This reminds me that we are not alone on this planet. There are other people, other countries, with other leaders, cultures, beliefs, and governments. Instead of criticizing those, acknowledge their existence, their devotion and dedication to their ideals and laws, cultural traditions, their rich history, and even their religions. Take a week to become aware of them and emphasize only the good, not the negative.

For years, some members of society have criticized Muslims—all Muslims. But they don't acknowledge that there are great Muslims in the world who are beautiful people. For a week, let's emphasize only the good. Again, the law of cause and effect would activate. Other nations, countries, cultures, and religions would feel the acknowledgment, and they would respond. The effect could impact the relationships between people, governments, and entire nations. They would be more responsive, as would we. Literally, this could shift the planet.

| Sacred Words to Use: | |
| --- | --- |
| • Culture | • Diversity |
| • Religion | • Spirituality |
| • Ethics | • Honor |
| • Dedication | • Tradition |
| • History | • Value |
| • Tolerance | • Acceptance |

Sacred Acknowledgements:

- The many cultures of the world are enriching and contribute to diversity and acceptance.

- Rather than avoiding the diversity of ethnicities, I embrace them.

- Christianity, Buddhism, Islam, Hinduism, Judaism, and New Age are religions to be recognized and acknowledged.

- The ethics followed by every country are to be respected.

- Every nation deserves to be commended for their beliefs and impact on the world as a whole.

- There is honor in every country's beliefs, traditions, religions, and principles.

- The dedication of religious leaders, including the Pope, pastors, ministers, priests, nuns, rabbis, and all other leaders is commendable and acknowledged.

- The rich history of all nations is valued as they all contribute to the enhancement of the universe and its cultures.

- I acknowledge all beliefs and societies and view them with tolerance and acceptance.

- Every faith deserves acknowledgment and praise.

- I acknowledge with admiration the traditions, celebrations, principles, and politics of nations across this great world.

- It is with deep acceptance that I acknowledge your country's contribution to the world.

- The greatness of the people in your nation and faith has benefitted so many.

## Chapter 12

# How to Acknowledge
# Leaders and Presidents

*How can you honor* your leaders and/or president? You may not agree with them, their issues, causes, and actions, but that doesn't mean you shouldn't honor their role and its importance on country and society. Theirs is a job of service to many—they cannot please all—but they should receive respect for following through on their promises, their commitment and loyalty to their nation, their willingness to listen and respect other views and perspectives, their desire to compromise for the good of all, and their public stature in society.

Failing to acknowledge or respect our leaders and presidents, would destroy our structure—and the respect for them and our laws and leaders. As a result, there would be chaos, and any semblance of unity would disappear, being replaced by darkness and destruction.

Acknowledging your leaders does not mean that you agree with all of their principles, ideals, or actions. It's more of a signal that you respect their role and its importance to our system of government. An acknowledgement in this manner could come in the form of a letter acknowledging their work, their votes, their principles, etc. You can acknowledge them for their commitment or dedication to what they believe is in the best interests of the people—even if you don't personally agree with some of their policies.

Other forms of acknowledgement to leaders and presidents are voting, volunteering, and communicating. Supporting to strengthen areas that you believe in is a great form of acknowledgement. Electing, either by voting and/or by supporting an individual who is running for public office, is another. Communicating, whether in an attempt to persuade another, offer a different opinion or perspective, or as a form of compromise or assistance is also an acknowledgement that you can make to leaders and presidents.

Leaders also have an incredible impact on others when they acknowledge them. For example, let's look at our country's presidents. They have an opportunity to create instant acknowledgement and connection. One person who was incredible and gifted in doing so was President Clinton. He created immediate connection and made people feel like they were the only one in the room, even in the midst of thousands of people. Whether he was in a small room or amongst thousands, he would instantly make them feel acknowledged and like they were the only one there. He gave the sincere impression that they mattered. As a result, he created a lifelong impression on the person.

Every person I have ever met who has met President Clinton has indicated they felt like there was nobody else there. I have experienced this. I study him when I see him on television, because he has that presence, an immediate presence, like looking you in the eye, even if it's for 10 seconds, and he forms a human connection that leaves you feeling like you were being seen, noticed, and recognized by him. You'll never forget the way he looked at you, and you'll assume that he'll never forget how he looked at you, either. I guarantee that he'll probably remember the face that belongs to every hand he shook.

That's how it feels when a person gives instant attention and acknowledgement; it's recognition. When someone feels like they're the only person in the room, they feel like a star. It makes them feel incredible.

Who and where is the person who can say the same about you, even if they don't know your name?

| **Sacred Words to Use:** | |
|---|---|
| • Country | • Loyalty |
| • Patriotism | • Dedication |
| • Commitment | • Representation |
| • Admiration | • Respect |
| • Gratitude | • Consideration |
| • Compromise | • Togetherness |

Sacred Acknowledgements:

- Be present in the moment with every person you meet, young or old.

- I acknowledge your selfless service and leadership to our country.

85

- Your loyalty is impressive and an example to all.

- You display such patriotism as you carry out your duties.

- I acknowledge the dedication in which you carry out your responsibilities as President (alderman, mayor, Sheriff, Chief, Senator, Representative, Governor, etc.).

- I acknowledge your devout commitment to improving the quality of life for your constituents.

- Your representation is admirable and a blessing.

- It is with admiration that I acknowledge the manner in which you communicate with the public.

- I acknowledge and respect your devotion in working on the public's behalf.

- It is with gratitude that I acknowledge you for choosing a career of service to others and your country/community.

- I acknowledge the consideration you have given to all opinions before determining your position.

- Only through compromise can positive changes occur. I acknowledge your patience and understanding when compromising for the good of all.

Ways to Acknowledge:

Voting, volunteering, communicating issues, listening with intent and purpose, contributing, displays of respect, etc.

## Chapter 13

# How to Acknowledge
# Thought Leaders

*Celebrities often support causes* and positions, charities, and other worthwhile venues. Their ability to reach a wide audience and bring vast exposure is massive. When they opt to use their position to spread a message or bring awareness, they should be commended and acknowledged. They don't have to do this—but by doing so, they are using their positions in a powerful, positive manner. They mobilize their audience around a shared vision.

Audrey Hepburn received the Presidential Medal of Freedom for her work as a UNICEF Goodwill Ambassador. Bono is a political activist. Angelina Jolie brought attention to the plight of refugees in countries across the world. Charlize Theron is an ambassador for peace and rape prevention. Nicole Kidman is an advocate for women's rights. Oprah Winfrey has supported a multitude of causes.

When thought leaders, celebrities, and other personalities commit publicly to a cause, they inspire others to do the same. They not only create awareness, but build a following and help raise funds. Their fans and followers gain a new understanding of issues. They do this due to strong beliefs and values. Should their message fall on deaf ears, they wouldn't be effective, but because of their unique ability to reach millions, they are very effective relayers.

Many celebrities have made a difference in the world. Oprah is one who is renowned the world over. Brad Pitt and Angelina Jolie created the awareness of making a difference in this world in different countries. To me, they are all heroes. I know they have the fortune to do what they do, but they don't do it for the acknowledgement. But that certainly doesn't mean that they should not be acknowledged for their efforts.

It's an honor to acknowledge these people and their contributions. Take the time to bring awareness to them—not only celebrities, but acknowledge everyone who makes a difference. Create a special day for them, just to acknowledge the goodness, unselfishness, and contributions they offer. There could be a special talk show devoted entirely to acknowledging them. Instead of television shows where hosts interview Chris Brown, bringing up what he did one time and focusing on the negative, a show could focus on the positive. Look what this person actually did with his life and how he turned his life around! Look how this person made a huge difference in somebody else's life! I guarantee, if you acknowledge him for what he did, he'll be giving 100 times more than he is giving already.

There are so many thought leaders to acknowledge. Mother Theresa devoted her life to others. Father Flanagan was a visionary. In founding Boys Town, he gave acceptance, love, and an education to many deserving young boys. Martin Luther King, Jr., was a thought leader who advocated for civil rights and equality. In doing so, he inspired and changed lives.

There is no shortage of thought leaders to acknowledge, and every day another one is born. By acknowledging them, their efforts, and their impact on the lives of others, you give them the support and recognition they so deserve.

| **Sacred Words to Use:** | |
| --- | --- |
| • Appreciation | • Gratitude |
| • Admire | • Donate |
| • Sharing | • Dedication |
| • Compassion | • Commend |
| • Respect | • Value |
| • Contribution | • Principles |

Sacred Acknowledgements:

- I acknowledge President Clinton and other major politicians who make the time and effort to let others know they are important.

- It is with gratitude that I acknowledge the unselfish service and devotion exhibited by Angelina Jolie, Oprah, and other celebrities who have made a positive impact on the lives of women and children around the globe.

- I admire those who use their public popularity to bring attention to worthy causes.

- Through their service and donation, celebrities who donate to charitable causes have made a profound impact on the world around them. I acknowledge them by making a donation.

- Acknowledging and sharing issues and solutions: By acknowledging issues and sharing them, thought leaders have benefitted the world and serve as role models.

- As an ambassador, the dedication you display in your role is worthy of praise.

- I acknowledge the compassion exemplified by artists and musicians by performing in concerts and events in order to raise awareness and funding toward worthwhile causes.

- I commend our President for using his position to inspire and motivate minorities to achieve their goals.

- It is with deep respect that I acknowledge our First Ladies for using their platform to raise awareness to causes that affect the citizens of our country and their desire to make a positive contribution to others.

- I value and acknowledge Oprah Winfrey for her generous donations, gifts, and unselfish nature.

- I acknowledge Ellen Degeneres for always being the gift to all who view her daily.

*Chapter 14*

# How to
# Acknowledge Mentors

*Mentors are truly unselfish.* They share their wisdom, experience, knowledge, and advice in order to help others improve and grow. They motivate, inspire, and provide support, tools, and connections to their mentees. Often, they do so, asking nothing in return. It is an act of selfless goodwill at no cost to those they mentor. Some people mentor one on one, in a face-to-face environment. Others offer virtual mentorship, communicating and sharing electronically or through other means. Some mentors are leaders—they write books, offer wisdom and advice via websites, audio, or video.

Mentors are often successful and experienced. They can be life or career coaches. They can be a parent, a relative, a teacher, a coach, or consultant. A mentor can even be a neighbor, a professional associate, or a friend.

Benjamin Graham mentored Warren Buffet. Steve Jobs' mentor was Robert Friedland.

Don Graham mentored Mark Zuckerberg, Facebook's founder.

Andrew Carnegie of Carnegie Steel mentored Charles Schwab.

Madonna mentored Gwyneth Paltrow.

Audrey Hepburn served as a mentor to Elizabeth Taylor.

Mel Gibson was Heath Ledger's mentor.

Even presidents and powerful world leaders had mentors. President Thomas Jefferson was mentored by George Mason. Mahatma Gandhi was the mentor to the late Dr. Martin Luther King, Jr. Gandhi also mentored Nelson Mandela. Mentoring goes back centuries— Socrates mentored Plato, and Plato mentored Aristotle.

You acknowledge the mentor the most by the result you create in your life. I don't think there's a better way to acknowledge a mentor than to thrive in life. And I say thrive. Besides that, you can also acknowledge a mentor by calling him or her or showing up on his or her doorstep—it could be with flowers, a note, or cookies—or send him or her a message or a text. However, remember that there is nothing better than a face-to-face acknowledgement. Of course, that's not always possible. Do it any possible way because their role and contribution to our future should not be taken for granted.

Often, the greatest acknowledgement of a mentor's impact on one's life and/or career is to use their advice and share it with others, passing along their contribution.

When acknowledging, express the importance of their support, advice, successes and failures, experiences shared, vision, connections, for accepting a responsibility to use their roles to enhance and help others.

**BEST MENTOR AWARD**

| **Sacred Words to Use:** | |
| --- | --- |
| • Wisdom | • Gratitude |
| • Knowledge | • Experience |
| • Insight | • Expertise |
| • Sharing | • Caring |
| • Sacrifice | • Generosity |

Sacred Acknowledgements:

- Your wisdom is invaluable.

- It is with gratitude that I acknowledge your willingness to devote time to my success every week.

- The knowledge you share is phenomenal and worth its weight in gold!

- The expertise you bring to the table is impressive.

- The insight you have provided in regard to financial security is incredible.

- The greatest acknowledgement I'd like to share with you is through sharing your teachings with others.

- I acknowledge that your lessons and advice were shared in such a caring and compassionate manner.

- The 25 years of experience you have truly enhance and enrich the advice you have shared.

- I understand the sacrifice you are making by taking the time to be my mentor. Please know it is not taken for granted.

- The generosity you exemplify by volunteering your advice and guidance speaks highly of your character and professional reputation.

# Chapter 15

# How to
# Acknowledge Friends

*Friends through thick and thin.* Some are new; some are old. Some last a short time, while others are lifetime gifts. Friends enrich your life, providing you with new perspectives and experiences. They contribute happiness, joy, comfort, compassion, and understanding to your life.

I think there is no better gift than to have friends for many years. The years speak for themselves when acknowledging a friend and the time spent together. I'm referring to time spent **together—time spent in the present, focused on each other.** Today, people are so busy looking through all Facebook and Twitter accounts, text messages, and the five different phones they're carrying that there is no longer time for human communication. Technology and the impersonal have taken the place of the personal and intimate relationship people can and should have with a real friend and confidante.

Actually spending time with a friend is not only just acknowledging the friend, but it is also acknowledging yourself. You can acknowledge friends in other ways, as well. Send him or her a note, expressing how special they are. Listen to them and be there, fully present, to hear what they have to say and how they feel. Remember, listening is a powerful acknowledgement. Listening and understanding are also key elements to the deepest friendships. Commit to visiting each other and develop traditions. Acknowledge their favorite flower, color, song, or season to let them know that you remember what is special in their life.

In short, don't take friends for granted. They are a unique gift with the most unique relationship. A friend is often irreplaceable, and for that reason alone, set aside time to value them in your life ... and let them know how valuable they are.

Acknowledging: Who is your oldest and/or dearest friend? Write down the qualities that attracted you to him or her and those that you admire.

List different friends: Coworkers, neighbors, best friends, associates, church friends, classmates, etc. Acknowledge them for their role in your life and the impact and contributions they have made, as well as the qualities of their character.

*We meet friends*
*for a reason,*
*a season,*
*or a lifetime.*

---

**Sacred Words to Use:**

- Trust
- Understanding
- Sharing
- Companionship
- Loyalty
- Encouragement
- Confidence
- Compassion
- Comfortable
- Devotion
- Friendship
- Support

Sacred Acknowledgements:

- The trust between us is one of the most valuable things about our relationship.

- Your confidence is impressive and deserving. What a great job you're doing!

- As my best friend, I couldn't ask for anyone more understanding.

- You are so compassionate. It makes me want to be like you.

- The flowers you grew in your front yard are a sight to behold. How wonderful of you to share them with the neighborhood.

- This has been a wonderful long talk. You have such a way of making people feel comfortable in sharing their lives with you.

- By shaving your head to support our dear friend in her fight against cancer, you have shown an incredible and impressive level of devotion.

- The mark of a true friend is in how loyal they are. You are a true friend.

- Please accept this photograph of our beach outing together as an acknowledgement of our friendship.

- Your encouragement couldn't have come at a better time! You have such a way with words!

- Please accept this donation as a symbol of support for the hard work you've done for our church this year. It has been noticed!

# Chapter 16

# How to
# Acknowledge Authors

*"Books are the quietest and most constant of friends;
they are the most accessible and wisest of
counselors, and the most patient of teachers."*
— Charles William Eliot

Whether books are read for enjoyment or information, they are indeed food for the mind and the soul. Books are the greatest wealth of knowledge available—and the most profound educational tool anyone will ever know. The authors of those books are sharing their unique experiences, their knowledge, their ideas, and the unique marriage of words to entertain, enlighten, and make others grow. Above all, they fuel the mind with curiosity and life.

Behind every great book is a great author. Acknowledge their contribution, the sharing of their wisdom and conveyance of their message. The works they leave behind are a legacy for all to enjoy for centuries to come.

Writing reviews for a book that changed your life could be an acknowledgement of an author. You could do something even more special and host a book reading party for the book and its author. Other ways to acknowledge authors would be to sell books for him or her, buy his/her books for friends, coworkers, or family, and highly recommend the author's works to others.

Start with a personal acknowledgement that you admired all the thoughtful things said, the knowledge, inspiration, entertainment, etc., you got out of reading the book. If you share that acknowledgement as a review, your opinion will impact others who are interested in the topic or book.

The more books an author sells, the more acknowledgement he or she gets. When you support the author, you help him or her become known and successful. You become part of the cause and effect. By being inspired by the author's words, you can now pay it forward and support others to become inspired, as well.

How, where, and when will you post and share the author's work, bring attention to their publication and share their inspiration? From testimonials to endorsements, recommendations and referrals, the greatest complement and achievement an author can receive is acknowledgement for their work and praise for the way they presented it.

---

**Sacred Words to Use:**

- Growth
- Awareness
- Entertaining
- Curiosity
- Expressions
- Contribution
- Insight

- Enlightenment
- Awakening
- Information
- Gratitude
- Grateful
- Wisdom
- Delightful

---

Sacred Acknowledgements:

- Napoleon Hill's bestselling book *Think and Grow Rich* has been an inspirational tool for the growth of many entrepreneurs.

- A work of artistry and enlightenment, everyone will enjoy reading this author's latest and greatest book!

- Chocked full of knowledge, perhaps this book's greatest accomplishment is the awareness it creates.

- After reading this book, you will experience an awakening that will make you rethink your former beliefs! Truly an eye-opening adventure!

- Nicholas Sparks has done it again with this story, which is a tale of history and entertainment.

- For those who want a firsthand portrayal of Lyme disease, look no further than this book, which is as easy to understand as it is informative.

- A mystery from first page to last, the author uses his gifts to pique his readers' curiosity throughout this tale.

- With gratitude for your delivery and timely message, I endorse your book. It will prove to be a resource for many students in their educational endeavors.

- What a way with words! You express yourself so eloquently. Know that I will gladly recommend your book to the members of my reading club!

- With a wisdom beyond his years, the author has found a way to bring new information to an age-old topic, making his reader ponder their previous beliefs.

# Chapter 17

# How to
# Acknowledge Pets

*Animals have a purpose,* from dogs that provide love and companionship, to security dogs, therapy dogs, Seeing Eye dogs, and dogs that detect seizures. There are also cats of all breeds, hamsters and gerbils, and birds, such as parakeets and canaries. Some people have pet snakes or potbelly pigs. They bring joy to our lives and become part of the family unit. Animals have a profound sensitivity to sound, smoke, heat, and have saved many lives by detecting things that are abnormal. They are also deeply loyal to their owners.

The pets you take into your home and heart get to be acknowledged. They have feelings and long to be included as part of the family unit. They desire many of the same things we do—food, warmth, comfort, and companionship. For their loyalty, work, admiration, and devotion, they deserve to be revered and to feel confident that their love is returned.

One way to acknowledge pets is simply to spend time with them. Take them outdoors for a walk. Play with them and give them the exercise they need to be healthy. Be attentive to their health and needs. Touch them and reward them for being good and being an integral and important part of your life. And because they give you so very much and ask so little in return, give them a special place of comfort that is their very own. They deserve it.

| **Sacred Words to Use:** | |
| --- | --- |
| • Companion | • Friend |
| • Comfort | • Love |
| • Play | • Appreciative |
| • Devotion | • Security |
| • Affection | • Obedient |
| • Gentle | • Beautiful |

Sacred Acknowledgements:

- You are the best companion ever! C'mon, let's go for a walk.

- I look forward to the time we spent together because you are such an unselfish and wonderful friend.

- Here, let me get your blanket and make you nice and comfortable.

- Oh, what a great kiss! I love you, too, little buddy.

- You've been such a good girl stuck inside all day; I bet you want to play. Fetch your ball!

- Oh, how I appreciate you! You're such a wonderful addition to our family.

- Look at you staying so close to the baby. Wow, how devoted you are!

- You always provide such great security, letting us know if you hear anything strange.

- Oh, you are the most affectionate little puppy!

- I can see how much self-discipline you have. You are one of the most obedient dogs I've ever known.

- What a gentle kitten you are! Here, come sit in my lap.

Yes—practice this and watch them respond!

# Chapter 18

# How to
# Acknowledge Neighbors

*Neighbors are the people* in your life who, by geography, have a window into your world and vice versa. You are families living near each other, and sometimes you become friends. If not, your children are friends with their children. Some of your earliest friends were your neighbors; you played together as children. In close proximity, you are able to witness their lives from a distant and personal vantage point. Your neighbors may be the people who live in the apartment across the hall or the family that lives on the farm one mile down the road. Because you are joined by location, they play a role in your life.

You may thank neighbors for their friendship and companionship, for lending you tools or a cup of flour, or for giving you a ride when you need it. They might lend a helping hand or extend congratulations or sympathies in your life's milestones. They may take care of your pets when you are gone or car pool your children. Some neighbors simply offer you privacy, giving you space without infringing on your life. Some respect boundaries and expect the same in return. Regardless, they know your routines and your name, and most people would feel free to call upon their neighbors for assistance, if necessary.

Acknowledging your neighbors is important. Earlier in this book, I mentioned that I brought a neighbor flowers because she kept a watchful eye on my property. We were not close, but the acknowledgement helped me to see her in a different way—I saw that she had feelings, emotions, and was touched by my simple gesture.

It's so beautiful to experience neighbors acknowledging you. Recently, I built a pond in my front yard. I did it for myself and then I realized that every neighbor would stop by and start talking to me because they felt acknowledged by me for giving this to the community. I was absolutely amazed how people came and acknowledged me for giving this gift. To be honest, I didn't build it for that reason. The more they gave me the acknowledgement, the more people, even when they drove up at one or two in the morning, there would be standing around and listening to the waterfall coming down.

I acknowledged the people by putting a bench outside. I bought a nice, new little bench because I figured they deserved to be able to sit and enjoy my pond. In reality, they acknowledged me and I acknowledged them for actually taking the time to enjoy what I built. A homeless man stopped by one day, and I said, "Why don't you come and sit and listen to the waterfall when you're in the neighborhood?" He was so thankful.

Acknowledge other people by giving. Acknowledge neighbors for taking care of the grass, by noticing something new in their yards, and driving through my neighborhood. I love my neighborhood chats and learning what my neighbors do and about events in their lives. It's a great way to discover how to keep the community going and informed, whether it's bad or good. I always let people know that I'm here and notice them and their contribution, because a lot of people may notice, but don't let anybody know that they value it. Let people know, and especially your neighbors, that you value them.

| **Sacred Words to Use:** | |
| --- | --- |
| • Friendship | • Companionship |
| • Support | • Security |
| • Privacy | • Assistance |
| • Helpfulness | • Respect |
| • Confidentiality | • Sharing |

Sacred Acknowledgements:

- I have noticed the friendship you extend to your neighbors. It is so kind of you to take the time to recognize and be a part of everyone's lives.

107

- The companionship you so faithfully extend to those who live around you is a gift to treasure.

- What a wonderful expression of support you gave to the Girl Scouts when they came around selling cookies!

- Your observance has given our neighborhood a sense of security that deserves recognition.

- I know there are times when neighbors can infringe on each other, but I commend you for always respecting the privacy of those who live near.

- You can always be counted on when assistance is needed—please know that is a rare and valued quality that is so appreciated!

- I acknowledge your kindness by shoveling our driveway after the snow last week. Your helpfulness while my husband was recovering from surgery will not be forgotten.

- I commend you for the way in which you treat your neighbors with such respect. It really makes a difference.

- Living in such close proximity makes it difficult not to know each other's lives. The confidentiality you've always shown is an admirable quality.

- The flag and pole you installed is so magnificent. What a great way to share your patriotism with the neighborhood!

## Chapter 19

# How to Acknowledge
# Past Loved Ones

*Past loved ones could* mean those who you once loved but who are no longer part of your life, such as a former boyfriend/girlfriend, former friends, etc. It could also be friends and family who have passed away and departed this life. Why should you acknowledge them? First, they have shaped you and contributed to who you are and the memories and experiences you will forever cherish. They might be a grandparent, parent, aunt, uncle, cousin, or sibling, or even a spouse or child. Acknowledging their impact on your life is a tribute to them and a way to keep them alive for generations to come.

How can you acknowledge them? By sharing memories and stories about them, revisiting photographs, visiting their gravesite, praying to them and for their souls, creating or contributing to memorials, attending memorial services, and donating to causes that were near and dear to their heart in their honor. Acknowledging people who are deceased is very individual and should focus on what you think is important, but acknowledging our past loved ones is always remembering them and mentioning them. There is a saying that expresses this well: "Remember him/her well and remember them often." That doesn't mean you should acknowledge them as if they are still alive. In a way, they are still alive—they are just in a different phase of their life. You now get to acknowledge them always for being there, even though you can't see them. By acknowledging them for being there, you will feel and experience their presence.

Acknowledging past loved ones in your meditations brings peace and acceptance, while making you still feel close to the ones you loved.

Professional athletes have been known to acknowledge a departed parent or grandparent before or after every game with a gesture to the heavens, a wave, a hand on the heart, etc. During an Oscar ceremony, some celebrities may acknowledge someone who has recently deceased. It happens often during award ceremonies; they always do it in memoriam of people who passed in the film industry.

Some ways to acknowledge past loved ones might be planting a tree in memory of the person. There are people who still set the table and acknowledge the presence that their loved one once had during meals. We can also acknowledge them by visiting a park that was special. Or we can simply acknowledge them for having helped us become the person we are. Acknowledge them for all the greatness and the thoughts they instilled in us.

Acknowledgment can also come in the form of scholarship funds or non-profits in their name. For instance, Amber Alert is an actual law that was created and named after an individual as an acknowledgment.

I personally have a non-profit in my mother's name. There are other opportunities to acknowledge someone and their legacy. For example, in a zoo that was being built, people could purchase a stone and have the name of a person engraved on that stone. You could buy something and donate it in your loved one's name. It's a way to keep their name alive while you're alive.

| **Sacred Words to Use:** | |
|---|---|
| • Memory/Memorial | • Cherish |
| • Treasure | • Peace |
| • Acceptance | • Love |
| • Tribute | • Testament |
| • Faith | • Legacy |
| • Heritage | • Lineage |

Sacred Acknowledgements:

- The new cancer wing of the hospital is being named for the vice president of the hospital, in memory of his continual efforts to be at the forefront of cancer treatments in the Midwest.

- Oh, the cherished memories you have left behind, especially here on this bench where we shared many warm and loving talks.

- Mom, you did such a wonderful job caring for your family. We will always treasure your love and the lessons you shared.

- Today's mass was dedicated to my father. It was such a beautiful message of peace and love and an acknowledgement of a life well lived.

- My sister displayed a calm acceptance of her diagnosis; in her memory, please accept this donation so that others may live.

- It is with deep and lasting love that I acknowledge and celebrate your birthday today with a slice of your favorite chocolate cake.

- In memory of my brother, I visited the monument in tribute of fallen soldiers.

- Honor: I am pleased to accept this award for my departed sister and her tireless work in honor of those less privileged.

- As a testament of love, this tree is being planted, where it will grow and serve to remind us of the beauty you brought into the world.

- Knowing that I will see you again in the next phase of life is the result of the faith you always had and generously shared with everyone you knew.

## Chapter 20

# How to
# Acknowledge Holidays

*In our culture, most* holidays are celebratory occasions, such as Christmas, New Year's, Easter, Fourth of July, Labor Day, Thanksgiving, etc. They are days when families and friends gather to celebrate with dinners, parties, picnics, or while attending church functions. Some holidays spark generosity and the satisfaction of giving to others, while others affirm relationships with family and friends—the people you want to be with and close to during these occasions.

The holiday season is so amazing because the spirit is in the air. The season makes people feel so special, and it's because it is the season and holiday of giving. How come we can't do this all the time? That's what this book is all about, to actually be in the holiday spirit every day, all year long.

Holidays are more than parties and presents, though; they can be sacred or patriotic. They can be about thankfulness or offer us a time of rest. They can bring cheer and goodwill into your world and give you an opportunity to acknowledge those who serve or help you, as well as those who bring happiness, joy, and love into your life.

Other cultures enjoy some of our holidays, but not all. Their acknowledgements may be different—with different traditions, foods, and expectations. Some of these occasions are celebratory and happy, while others are serious, humble, and an opportunity to bestow honor upon people, places, or higher beings.

Regardless of the holiday and how it is celebrated, holidays hold a special place and purpose. They provide opportunities to acknowledge and celebrate that which is important to you. Giving a gift, especially a thoughtful one, is one way to acknowledge a holiday and the person who will receive the gift. Another is to attend events connected to the holiday, such as concerts, tributes, memorials, family gatherings, and church masses. Still another is to volunteer to help or serve others during holidays. For example, helping cook or serve a Thanksgiving dinner for those who do not have a family or a traditional meal, or caroling during the Christmas season to bring cheer to neighbors. The holidays present so many ways for you to acknowledge them. You are only limited by your imagination.

How can you bring the holiday spirit into your life and the lives of your loved ones on a daily or weekly basis? Don't wait for a calendar holiday!

| **Sacred Words to Use:** | |
|---|---|
| • Cheer | • Goodwill |
| • Celebrate | • Prayer |
| • Gathering | • Generosity |
| • Honor | • Peace |
| • Joy | • Sharing |

Sacred Acknowledgements:

- Enjoy this bottle of champagne and toast to the cheer of another day!

- As a sign of goodwill, volunteering every Monday at the Salvation Army is a privilege.

- This Christmas gives us yet another reason to celebrate with our family and enjoy time together.

- Before Easter brunch, let us say a prayer for the feast before us and the gift of time that we have together.

- Family gatherings are not reserved solely for major holidays; Sunday dinners are my favorites.

- Please accept this gift from my family to yours for the generosity you've always shared with your extended family.

- The entire family is attending mass this Sunday with Mom, thankful for the fact that we can all get together to celebrate her 85th birthday in a meaningful way.

- Please enjoy these egg rolls; they are made for you in Honor of the Chinese New Year.

- His eulogy was a message of peace that stayed with everyone throughout the day.

- What's the special occasion? There isn't one! There is so much joy when we get together. This picnic is simply for fun.

*Chapter 21*

# How to Acknowledge
# Art and Creativity

*Creativeness is a gift* everyone possesses, but in different ways. Some have to ignite their creativity, while others may need to help it grow. Some people are naturally gifted and being creative is part of their life. Creativity could mean the ability to think differently and create new methods, policies, or solutions. It could also be the ability to see something in a different way, to find a different use for a common item or a way to improve its functionality. It could be the ability to create something unique entirely from the imagination. Being creative for some might be the ability to weave a story of fiction in such a way that it captures attention and sparks emotions. It could be a child's first drawing or an award-winning masterpiece like the Mona Lisa. Drawing, painting, sculpting, and designing are all creative endeavors, and the art that such creators bring into the world brings beauty to our homes, our neighborhoods, workplace, institutions, and landscapes.

There are so many artists in the world. The biggest acknowledgement for an artist is to have people show up when they showcase their gifts. There's no better acknowledgement than when people come to an exhibit to see their art. And, of course, there is no better acknowledgement than if somebody actually buys it and is willing to pay the asking price for its worth.

How else can you acknowledge art? It all comes down to your own self-worth and your own awareness, because when it comes to art, it's really hard to say this one thing should be $1 million, another should be $1,000, and yet another should be free. I have seen a Picasso that brought about this remark, "That should be free. If you gave it to me, I wouldn't want it."

So art is in the eye of the beholder. Can you truly acknowledge that person for whatever they saw in their creation, letting them know that it is amazing, even if you don't see it through their eyes? Acknowledge them for their creativity and their willingness to spend their time to produce and share it with others.

Acknowledging art and creativity opens you up to beauty. You'll become more aware of it in your life and home, and by acknowledging it, you'll strengthen your capacity to appreciate and create it at a deeper level.

---

**Sacred Words to Use:**

- Creativity/Creation
- Imagination
- Awe
- Gift / Gifted
- Unique
- Stunning
- Beauty
- Wonder
- Invention
- Emotional
- Talent
- Admiration

Sacred Acknowledgements:

- What an amazing creation! The jewelry you design is a statement of your incredible style.

- Bobby, the picture you drew in class today shows what a wonderful imagination you have.

- The landscape you painted is a work of beauty. I can picture myself being there.

- You are so talented! Your animated cartoon is a work of wonder and amazement that is sure to delight so many children!

- I am in awe of the creativity it took in designing your new home.

- Your invention is inspirational. It will benefit so many people.

- The painting you gave me is a reflection of your incredible gift.

- That song is just astounding. The lyrics you wrote are so emotional and heartwarming.

- Wow! I heard you were good, but the depth of your talent is shocking!

- Oh, my! The wedding dress you designed and sewed is stunning! How beautiful it is on you!

- Oh, I could stare at the paintings from the high school art class on display at the Civic Auditorium all day. They are each such a unique expression of talent.

## Chapter 22

# How to
# Acknowledge Beauty

*Beauty is indeed in* the eye of the beholder. It is true that beauty is individually defined and a matter of cultural and ethnic background, experience, and taste.

Beauty can be within, from the inside, and it can be on the outside, such as physical appearances. It can be in a person or in a panoramic sunset, a majestic mountain view, or in the interior design of a space. Beauty can be a feeling, such as love, i.e., their love is a beautiful thing to witness. It can be a sleek new sports car or a gleaming restored Model T. Beauty can be seen in the young and old, the weak and strong, and in personalities.

Beauty brings you a sense of true appreciation for things that you marvel at and admire. It can be the initial source of love and friendship. When you acknowledge the beauty that surrounds you and touches your life, you validate it and ensure that you will not take it for granted. A bonus—the more beauty you acknowledge, the more beauty you invite into your world and are able to see.

If it's beauty of the world or what you see outside, I think the best acknowledgement is to preserve it. Don't destroy the earth with litter and graffiti. Even if it's a car, become aware that there is a person next to you in their car and acknowledge the beauty of their car by trying not to put a dent in it. Be conscious when opening doors to avoid knocking a mirror off another car. That isn't hard to do; it's the right thing to do. It is about respecting that which is around you, even if you don't personally see the beauty in it. For example, a single mother recently was able to purchase a car so she could drive to and from work in order to support her family. The car is old and looks every bit of its age. However, the vehicle is reliable and a necessity that removed a hardship from their lives. While another person might look at the car and not see its beauty, there is no doubt that the single mother likely thinks that the car is a beautiful thing in her life.

Become aware and acknowledge and appreciate the beauty that surrounds you.

---

### Sacred Words to Use:

- Majestic
- Breathtaking
- Love
- Awe
- Beautiful
- Elegance
- Stunning
- Wonder/Wonderful
- Admire
- Attraction
- Appreciation
- Splendor

Sacred Acknowledgements:

- The mountains are simply majestic and a gift from nature.

- You have such timeless beauty; it is classic and stunning.

- The sunset this evening is breathtaking. I wish everyone could pause a minute to experience it.

- It was wonderful of the park district to install recycle bins, reminding us to care for our environment.

- From sea to shining sea, there is just so much to love and appreciate just beyond the horizon.

- The hard work put into restoring that Model A is to be admired. How wonderful to bring such a piece of history to life again!

- Oh, the love in a new mother's eyes is a thing of awe.

- Your physical beauty was the source of my initial attraction, especially your beautiful eyes.

- It may not be the Taj Mahal, but it is ours, and I'm thankful for a place to call home.

- By creating the sun, moon, earth, and seas, God also gave us a sense of appreciation for His creation.

- I chose these flowers because their petals look so delicate. They are a display of nature's elegance.

## Chapter 23

# How to
# Acknowledge Youth

*From infancy, youth is* sacred. Newborns are gentile and fragile, yet able to illicit strong feelings of love and pride. As you grow from birth, you are constantly learning. Your mind and body are being molded and shaped by the world around you. It's a state of newness and limitless possibilities. In your school years, you develop social skills and friendships and explore and discover interests and talents. You form your personality and expressions, with the freedom to do so. You are dependent, but striving to become independent as you learn and become responsible. In your teens and 20s, you are still in a state of discovery, seeking happiness, while finding your place in the world. The possibilities are abundant.

Youth is a time of energy, exploration, discovery, and growth. It is when you develop a sense of belonging and cultivate your interests. For most, these are the years that shape their beliefs about themselves and the world around them.

Children bring joy, laughter, happiness, and love into the lives of others. They are dynamic, unique, and vibrant. Their minds are a clean slate, ready to be written on and molded. Their bodies are growing, but are strong and enduring. The young spark our nurturing and protective instincts.

Because children are in their formative years and are so vulnerable to the opinions of others, it is important to provide them with positive acknowledgment. The main things children want to hear is that the people they care about are proud of them. Every child, regardless if they are young or an adult, wants to know that their parents are proud of them.

I've worked with that concept all of my life and have firsthand witnessed thousands of people when they hear their parents say, "I'm proud of you." It is the ultimate acknowledgement you can say to your children and to our youth.

Children also need to be told and reassured that they are good enough, right now, just the way they are. It's so wonderful for a child to know that a parent isn't focusing on the things the child cannot do. Instead, parents should focus and acknowledge the things a child is doing and can do—and that is everything.

**Sacred Words to Use:**

- Love
- Devotion
- Dependence
- Learning
- Wonder
- Exploration
- Laughter

- Affection
- Trust
- Energy
- Growth
- Fascination
- Joy
- Play

Sacred Acknowledgements:

- I love you just the way you are. Don't change a thing about yourself!

- There is so much affection between a parent and child. It's so touching to see.

- Your devotion to your schoolwork is impressive. You're doing a great job.

- It's okay to ask for help. Your dependence on others is a sign of trust.

- I'm amazed at the level of energy you have! You go, girl!

- Learning is a gift, and I'm more than happy to help you in any way I can.

- Taking care of you and watching you grow has helped me grow, too. Your growth and maturity are inspirational.

- Oh, how tiny and precious you are! You fill my heart with wonder every time I look at you.

- Your fascination with everything new is amazing.

- Take time to play and discover, little one. These are your formative years, so don't miss a thing!

- Having you in our family has filled our world with exploration and awe.

- Your laughter is contagious! What a joy it is to see you so happy!

- No, I'm not busy. There is nothing I would rather do right now than play with you.

*Chapter 24*

# How to Acknowledge
# Growing Older

*For some, it is dreaded,* but old age has its benefits. In some countries and cultures, it is fiercely respected and revered. Elders are considered a gift, with abundant wisdom and experience, and are treasured and respected by family members and society.

With age comes a gift—the gift of wisdom and experience. As people grow older, they not only have made mistakes, but also have learned from them—something that education cannot teach. They become wiser, knowing, and are able to see past passionate emotions to the core issues or causes. At this stage in life, there is peace and acceptance. There is a lifetime of experience and memories. While the body slows down, the aged mind is at its best, and they become the bearer of wisdom and information.

According to a study conducted by the University of Illinois, people are happiest in old age. They are also better able to resolve conflicts and find solutions. Because they have a wealth of knowledge and experience, they make fewer errors and are considerably more accurate in their endeavors. They are able to better appreciate different viewpoints and their keen social skills create a time in their life that is peaceful and drama free.

The beauty of life is that you actually get to acknowledge your old age just because you are fortunate to become a certain age. Many people were not that fortunate. That is nothing to be ashamed of and no reason to pretend or lie about your age. How silly is it to pretend to be younger than you really are? Who are you fooling? So acknowledge it; when you do, you are acknowledging the other person and acknowledging yourself.

On a day-to-day basis, you can make a daily acknowledgement valuing your years. For instance, "I'm still walking; I'm still talking; my mind is okay. I am good." Acknowledge your mind, that it's actually becoming stronger. Sure, you may have a senior moment, but it happens to all of us, even younger people. But if you actually say, "My mind is getting stronger and stronger; it's amazing. I know so much more now than I ever did. I'm getting better with age."

It's also so incredible to acknowledge the age of your elders. "I acknowledge your wisdom. Yeah, rub some of it off on me."

Remember, it's the grace of God that allows you to become that age. By itself, that is beautiful. Acknowledge those who are growing older gracefully and with beauty. Acknowledge yourself and your age as a positive.

*"We live in a youth-obsessed culture that is constantly trying to tell us that if we are not young, and we're not glowing, and we're not hot, that we don't matter. I refuse to let a system or a culture or a distorted view of reality tell me that I don't matter. I know that only by owning who and what you are can you start to step into the fullness of life. Every year should be teaching us all something valuable. Whether you get the lesson is really up to you."*
—Oprah,
*O, the Oprah Magazine*, May 2011

What does growing older mean for you? Write it down and acknowledge it!

---

**Sacred Words to Use:**

- Respect
- Blessing
- Knowledgeable
- Admire
- Aspire
- Satisfaction
- Contentment

- Fulfillment
- Knowing
- Experience
- Revere
- Grateful
- Dignity
- Sophistication

---

Sacred Acknowledgements:

- I acknowledge your vast experience and respect the wisdom you share with others.

- I'm getting older, and as I do, I find that my life has a greater sense of purpose and fulfillment. What a gift!

- Oh, to grow old is a blessing. I will embrace it with dignity.

- The older I am, the more knowing I become. It's great to know I'm getting smarter every year!

- I look to my elders for knowledge. Their life experience brings knowledge that cannot be found in books and schools.

- Your years of experience are impressive. I cannot wait to hear more of your stories.

- I've always admired you, Grandpa. You are an amazing source of wisdom.

- Age is to be revered, not dreaded. I'm getter better with every year!

- The grace you portray aspires me to be more like you. It is beautiful to witness.

- Rather than dreading turning 60, I am approaching it with a sense of gratefulness for all that life has given me thus far and anticipation of all that is to come.

- One of the benefits of growing older is that I can now sit back and enjoy the satisfaction of knowing I've accomplished so much.

- With old age comes a sense of dignity, one that can only be gained over time and through firsthand experience. I acknowledge the dignity, grace, and compassion in which you live your life.

- I acknowledge my great sense of humor, my drive, and passion to take a stand for other people's dreams and all their possibilities.

## Chapter 25

# How to Acknowledge
# Police, Military, and Firefighters

*It takes a special* courage and desire to protect and serve to become a police officer, service member, or firefighter. They put their lives on the line with each call or assignment. Sometimes offering assistance can be dangerous, but they are the first to do so in the call of duty. Sometimes providing safety and security to others means putting themselves in danger. This is true for those who protect our freedoms, fight for our honor and valor, and those who patrol our streets and provide immediate aid and assistance to us and our homes. Without law and order and those who are willing to sacrifice and risk their wellbeing, we would be a land of conflict and turmoil. Laws would be ignored and our liberties would be destroyed.

It's common to take the services of those who keep you safe for granted—until you need them. You know that 911 is there if you call, but how easy it is to forget how important their presence and service are until you have an accident, need assistance, or protection. People take for granted their freedoms and liberties, until their country is threatened ... or they see other countries being invaded.

Acknowledging is a way to express your appreciation for the presence, courage, training, and willingness of police officers, service members, and firefighters who protect and serve you every day. Acknowledge them for their valor, honor, and dedication and bless them and their families. Their safety is at the core of yours, and their role in your life and in the future of your country cannot be understated.

Acknowledge your belief that they protect and serve, even though sometimes you don't understand their method. Acknowledge those who are police officers, as well as those who would like to be police officers, because it's not a job that everyone wants to do. Where others are not willing to go, they are willing to go. Acknowledge them for the fact that every morning when they wake up, they go out into the world and risk their life.

The same is true for the military. Regardless of the reason a person joins the military, they are willing to make sacrifices and do fight for freedom—for other people's freedom and your freedom. That should be one of our biggest acknowledgements—because they are heroes.

One example of such an acknowledgement is the acknowledgement of fallen soldiers. I saw a display in an airport where they had pictures of men and women who had died. It was so moving and even included letters from their children. Obviously, it seems that people often acknowledge soldiers after they serve and die, rather than while they are serving.

Yet, it isn't difficult to acknowledge the military while they are alive and need to hear it. Write them letters. Send them a care package or inspirational card. Do something special for all of the soldiers everywhere. And do not to forget to acknowledge those who have served in prior years. They may no longer be in the service and did not die for their country, but they're alive, and they're suffering. They're in pain. They might have no limbs left. What have we done for them lately? Are you even aware that they exist? What can you do to acknowledge them and their families, who all suffer from the effects of post-traumatic stress? How can you let them know that they matter—that their service and sacrifice have not gone unnoticed or unappreciated?

---

### Sacred Words to Use:

- Honor
- Service
- Protect
- Safety
- Character
- Respect
- Sacrifice
- Valor
- Courage
- Bless
- Sacred
- Strength
- Patriotism
- Bravery

---

Sacred Acknowledgements:

- Attending the service for our veterans is an honor. I wouldn't miss it for the world.

- Please accept this token of appreciation for the valor in which you have served. Our country is better because of you.

- Your service has not gone unnoticed. I hope our letters and emails make it easier for you and the news from home brings you a sense of belonging until you return.

- Every day, you and your fellow volunteer firefighters display remarkable courage as you carry out your duties. Please accept this donation as a small token of appreciation for all you do.

- It is a selfless career to protect the public. I pray for your safety every day.

- Bless all who serve and protect us, for they have chosen a noble path and a valiant cause.

- As you strive to ensure the safety of the public, we will pray for your own safety.

- I know it wasn't easy, but what a sacred honor it was that you were chosen to accompany your fellow soldier home and return him to his family and loved ones. God bless you.

- The character you displayed in difficult circumstances is remarkable. Please accept this gift card with the hope that it will lighten your load and ease your burdens.

- Your job is not an easy one. It requires a special kind of strength. I hope this book inspires you to remain strong until you are able to return to the loving arms of your family.

- I give up my seat, place my hand over my heart, and applaud returning soldiers and veterans as a sign of my respect for their service.

- Placing a wreath on the grave of a veteran or fallen soldier on Memorial Day is an acknowledgment of their service and the patriotism they had for their country.

- I acknowledge you for the gift you are to this world.

- You are so appreciated and loved in our neighborhood. My kids are inspired to be like you when they grow up.

- The world is a better place because you're in it.

## Chapter 26

# How to Acknowledge
# Service Providers

*Your life is made* easier in so many ways by people who perform routine services. They are the people who carry the mail, pick up your trash, and deliver your daily newspaper. They might include a gardener, housekeeper, lawn service, babysitter or nanny, hairdresser or barber, or insurance agent. The role they play is often taken for granted, but it is one you depend on. They provide convenience, assistance, advice, guidance, and services that you need or want and should not be taken for granted.

Often, people fail to notice these people. When they do, it is their job that is focused on. Sometimes people talk down to service providers, including waiters or servers, gardeners or housekeepers. I'd like to acknowledge them for doing the job they are doing. Maybe they chose that job, but perhaps they had no other choice. I know people who were lawyers in other countries who now deliver pizza in the United States. Acknowledge these people because you really don't know where they've come from and the reason they're doing this job. It's not because the job is less than; no, it is equal. Acknowledge people as your equal. How incredible would that be? In addition, acknowledge them for their willingness to perform the duties required of their position. They provide necessary services, often under less than favorable conditions. Be grateful for them.

---

**Sacred Words to Use:**

- Service
- Assistance
- Dedication
- Helpfulness
- Professionalism
- Worthy
- Value

- Helpful
- Convenience
- Assistance
- Commitment
- Dependable
- Praise
- Grateful

---

Sacred Acknowledgements:

- I just wanted to stop by and let you know that the service you provide is appreciated. You do such a great job taking care of my garden that I was inspired to buy you a beautiful bouquet of flowers for a change.

- You have been so helpful. It's great to know that my children are in such trusting hands while I'm gone.

- The entrée recommendations you shared were fabulous! Please accept this tip for a job well done!

- Your flexibility in scheduling has been a much-needed convenience. If there is anything I can do to return the favor, please let me know.

- I see you delivering mail every day, whether it's raining, snowing, or blazing hot. That's dedication! Can I offer you a cold bottle of water or iced tea to carry on your route?

- I can always count on you to get in touch! You are such a committed insurance agent. I'm so glad we found you!

- As a healthcare provider, you carry your duties out with such professionalism. Here's a little something to brighten your day.

- One of the things I admire most about you is that you are dependable. May I refer your services to my friends and family?

- Your profession is worthy of praise. The park is so much more beautiful as the result of your maintenance.

- How wonderful it is to have dinner delivered to the door on a stormy night like this! Here is a little extra tip—be safe out there!

- Please accept this card as an acknowledgement of the service you provide. Know that I and others are grateful to know we can count on your services.

- I admire the professionalism in which you carry out your duties. You are a mature young man, and the yard work you've done for me has been outstanding.

*Chapter 27*

# How to
# Acknowledge Color

*Color brings vibrancy and* diversity to our lives. It affects our moods, sparks energy, or calms the soul. Color fuels our imagination and creativity. It transforms our world from bland to grand. Our personalities are expressed in color, and colors often stand for something.

In color psychology, green represents balance and growth. Red stimulates and is an energetic color. Blue represents peace, trust, and loyalty. Imagination is represented by the color purple. Pink represents love and femininity. Brown is serious, yet friendly. Gray signifies compromise. Yellow is sunny and vibrant. White represents wholeness, purity, and perfection, as well as innocence. Black is mysterious and the color of the unknown. Those representations may or may not hold true for you, for it is a fact that often the effect a color has on an individual is based on their past experiences.

The colors of your workplace and home set your moods and represent distinct personalities and purposes in each space. The colors of the outdoors, brown, blue, and green, bring balance and peace to your life.

The color of your clothing can also set the tone—bright colors represent creativity and fun, while subdued, neutral colors are favored for professionalism. The color of your skin must be included in this acknowledgement. The world is full of people with different skin colors, and many varied shades of those colors. Each is special and shares a unique genealogy, culture, and ethnic background.

Acknowledging the color around you empowers both you and the color. It enhances its ability to affect your mood, creativity, productivity, and personality.

Be grateful for all the colors in your world. Color is something easily taken for granted. Imagine a world without color. We would all sit in the same color all day. Wow, how boring. I could look at you and everything would be the same—colorless eyes, hair, skin, and clothes.

You choose your clothes for their color because certain colors accent others, and some colors enhance your beauty. Sometimes, you select colors for your home, car, wardrobe, etc., because they lift you up. Some colors bring you down. What colors give you more energy? What colors make you calm and relaxed? Acknowledge color and become aware of the colors you surround yourself with. Then you can use color in a positive way— by knowing how specific colors affect you, you can use color to create balance.

Color is a key element in a country's flag, and each color represents something. Color is also said to be an important component in a business—from the logo to the décor and advertising, the color creates an identity that should resonate with the target audience.

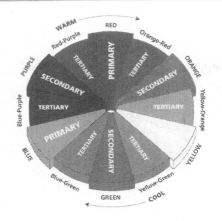

## Sacred Words to Use:

- Hue
- Vibrant
- Calm
- Tone
- Warm/Cold
- Happy
- Influence
- Shade
- Peaceful
- Energizing
- Mellow
- Inviting
- Rejuvenating
- Mood

Sacred Acknowledgements:

- Hue: Color not only brings diversity to life, but each one graces the world with multiple hues that enhance the world even more!

- From soft to bold, the many shades of color in this painting are spectacular!

- What a vibrant and magnificent mixture of color and textures there is in this pattern. I could stare at it all day.

- The spectacular display of colors in the sunset is always a peaceful sight to behold.

- Green always attracts me when I need to relax. Sitting in a park, surrounded by green grass and trees is so calming.

- Nothing is more energizing than a rainbow. Suddenly, its arch of colors makes the world seem so fresh and new.

- I look to color for balance and variety in my life. It can change the tone of an entire room instantly.

- On a cold evening, mellow colors call me, inviting me to relax in their warmth.

- The color of these flowers reminded me of you. They are so warm and inviting, just like you!

- I enjoy sitting in my office. The colors are warm and inviting. They influence my thoughts and attitude and help me create a productive and rewarding day.

- How can one not help but feel so terrifically happy in the presence of such a sunshiny yellow?

# Chapter 28

# How to
# Acknowledge Music

*Virtually every culture has* music. Music has been a part of mankind's expressions for the last 50,000 years. In history, music is of great importance. In the old countries, there has always been music, including tribal music that became a ritual and a vital part of a tribe's life and culture. Musical interests and tastes evolve and change over time, but the love for music has grown stronger. People listen to music at home, at the gym, in the car, and at work. Music provides the background for movies as it sets the scene, increasing the drama or calming the soul. Hospitals have found health benefits from playing music. Studies have shown that babies in the womb benefit from music and it has the capacity to increase or slow their heart rate and movements.

For some, music is a spiritual expression. For others, it is entertainment. Singing and playing a musical interest helps to develop the brain. Music reduces stress, motivates, eases pain, and improves cognitive performance and memory. Slow music can alter the speed of brainwaves, actually inducing meditative states. Fast music can make people feel upbeat and more energetic and productive. Music can increase passion, and it can trigger tears. Certain songs become representative of their cultures, such as national anthems; instruments can represent places or religions, such as an organ in church. The wedding march is viewed as a celebratory song, and a lullaby is a tender song that soothes and comforts.

Music sets the soul, especially when sacred words are used in the music. It comes from the spirits. I think we do honor music, without actually realizing that's what we're doing. Every time you put on your favorite song, you're acknowledging it, as well as what was within you. Look at what music strikes you—is it rap, or is it classical, rock, or country? Start listening truly to the messages of the music or the beat of the music.

Music is very, very powerful. Beethoven couldn't hear. Yet, notice the music he created.

What music lifts your spirit? You can acknowledge your spirit with the music you're going to play today. Who else can you play music for? You can acknowledge somebody you know or love with a special song or a special piece of music. Let the music for the day help the soul express itself.

For many, music has a season. Personally, I always sing *Jingle Bells* through the whole year, and when I sing *Jingle Bells,* good things happen. When I'm looking but can't find a parking place, I sing *Jingle Bells*, and, voila!, I have a parking place. Music is that powerful—become aware of the impact it has on you, and you will give it an opportunity to lift your spirits even higher.

## Sacred Words to Use:

- Beat
- Melody/Melodic
- Passion
- Harmonic
- Symbolic
- Moving
- Mood
- Entertaining
- Tune
- Soothe
- Energizing
- Spiritual
- Rhythm
- Soulful
- Enjoyment
- Enriching

Sacred Acknowledgements:

- The beat of the music is so moving I can feel it in my heart, almost like they're synchronizing.

- When different sounds are in tune and harmony, my life feels like it is in harmony, as well.

- Oh, the soft, sweet melody of the harp—it's so spiritual and moving.

- Sweet little baby, maybe a lullaby will soothe you to sleep.

- Wow, the music is so passionate, I can't help but feel charged.

- This song energizes me; I always play it when I need to get work done.

- The organ is such spiritual instrument; its chords speak to the heavens.

- The Star Spangled Banner stirs such patriotic feelings that it brings tears to my eyes.

- The bongos are symbolic of ancient tribal dances and rituals. I can almost feel myself being there witnessing their glorious traditions.

- The rhythm of the blues always evokes sadness, mixed with such a strong and unique culture. You play it so well that I can't help but feel emotional and caught up in it.

- Isn't it amazing how music brings balance to our lives? It is so powerful in healthcare, replacing anxiety with relaxation.

- This song is so soulful. I wanted to share it with you and let you experience how moving it is, too.

- You are like a symphony,

- You are a walking symphony.

- Your genius in listening to each note has created this track of music that is being listened to and enjoyed worldwide.

*Chapter 29*

# How to
# Acknowledge Seasons

*Every season has a* beginning and an end. Each offers rejuvenation and rest. The seasons of the year are a cycle that feed into each other, bringing climate change, as well as changes to nature and the earth that create food, beauty, abundance, activities, sports, shelter, and life.

Spring is a sign of renewal and growth as plants and trees come out of hibernation in response to the warmer temperatures. Summer is a time of bounty and harvest, when the sun feeds the growth of fruits and vegetables that will be harvested in the fall. Fall is crisp, with cooler air, and winter brings cold air, depending on one's climate and location, and snow and/or ice that melt in the spring to begin the cycle once again.

The seasons provide different activities and opportunities. Some people have seasonal work—outdoor jobs, farming, construction, etc. Some people have seasonal hobbies, such as gardening or hiking, skiing, swimming. Sports are also seasonal, with football beginning in the fall, baseball in the spring and summer, and basketball and hockey in the winter.

Most important, each season is an expression of beauty. Each offers a distinct landscape, green and warm, rustic with earthy tones, bright with new green foliage and spring and summer florals.

When I just came to this country and was working in a beauty salon, I was doing someone's hair when I heard the song, *I'll be Home for Christmas.* I was almost finished with the lady's hair, and she looked beautiful, but I started crying when I heard that song, and she started crying harder than I did. That song really had a significant impact on my life. The people I worked for noticed I was crying and asked what was going on. The lady said, "Oh, I was crying and she wants to be home for Christmas." One guy said, "My girl, why don't you go to the front desk and call the airlines and ask how much it costs to fly home for Christmas in the next couple of days? You won't be so heartbroken anymore." He was right. I did call, but the ticket was so expensive at the time I couldn't afford it. But at least I tried.

That is just one example of the seasons and how they impact lives. Over the holidays, acknowledge the season by visiting friends and family members and decorating your home, inside and out, to reflect the season. Some even follow certain customs, like spring cleaning, to rejuvenate their homes and make everything fresh and new again, like the outdoors. Also, acknowledge people with gifts and/or cards during the holidays. I sent my doctor gifts for Christmas.

Who is it that you can acknowledge around the holidays or different seasons of the year and life for what they did the whole year for you? It's very important that people become aware of that, as well. It's not just about the season or the holiday, but acknowledging others and letting them know you have appreciated them all year and are now, during this season, letting them know.

---

### Sacred Words to Use:

- Healing
- Celebration
- Customs
- Awakening
- Renewal
- Reflection
- Appreciation
- Transformation
- Traditions
- Growth
- Abundance
- Rejuvenating

---

Sacred Acknowledgments:

- I acknowledge the healing and rest that winter brings. Nature sleeps, heals, and refuels before spring.

- Christmas is a wonderful time to show appreciation for your kindness and friendship.

- Since our family reunion is held every Fourth of July, it is a wonderful celebration of our country's birthday and our family's closeness.

- I acknowledge the transformation power of spring and the opportunities it brings for change and growth as we clean out the old and start fresh and new.

- New Year's is more than a celebration; let's take time together this year to use it as a reflection on the last year and our appreciation for everything it brought into our lives.

- Visiting Grandma at the nursing home on her birthday is a custom our whole family follows in her autumn years.

- Please join us for our annual neighborhood football and bonfire celebration!

- Please enjoy these tulips. I hope you enjoy the awakening of their spring blooms as much as I do every year.

- I look forward to the school season. It is a time of growth and learning.

- The harvest season serves as a reminder of the abundance that surrounds us and graces our tables, homes, and lives. Let's share in its bounty together.

- **Spring:** Take a moment to acknowledge and admire the new leaves on the trees, the buds on the flowers, the birth of young birds and animals, and the presence of animals that have come out of hibernation.

- **Summer:** Acknowledge the sunshine for its warmth, light, and energy.

- **Fall:** Acknowledge the rain, the cool autumn air, the crispness and color of the falling leaves.

- **Winter:** Acknowledge the snow, ice, hail, and cold for their contribution to the earth and their scenic beauty.

Chapter 30

# How to
# Acknowledge History

*The past has always* played a pivotal role in the future. What you are today and the progresses you have made are due to past people, inventions, events, experiences, ideas, traditions, and beliefs. You should honor and respect those and avail ourselves of the rich education they offer. By learning from the past and applying it to the present, you gain appreciation for the contributions that have been made and the experiences that have shaped you.

History is a broad word, containing inventions, ideas, struggles, accomplishments, triumphs, failures, wars, famine, and feast. From politics and wars to entrepreneurial successes, the past has shaped your life. Movements have brought with them rights and liberties, recognitions, changes in your role at work, home, and in society. They have opened opportunities that were once closed. History has brought new technologies, role models, concepts, and remarkable people and contributions. Learning about these enriches your life and appreciation for what you do have, as well as your awareness of what you can accomplish.

In my historical tradition, every year I do something special and acknowledge myself. This is part of my legacy. It has become part of my life to create my own history—my own legacy. Part of my legacy is to give back. The first time I gave to charity, I was very young. Leprosy was prevalent at the time. I wanted to give where I knew it could make a difference. I thought about donating to cancer, but I didn't know if there was one person who would get better because I donated. However, on television, I learned that for $250 one person with leprosy could afford a doctor and become healthy. Every year, I donated and I also started fundraising.

I donated through the zoo, as well. I studied and became certified through the zoo to be a docent. I taught ages 5-16 by taking them through the zoo and loved it. For four years, I guided all the young kids through the zoo and taught them about zoology and all the animals. It was all part of my effort to give back. Eventually, I started the Torch Foundation to make a difference with youth. In addition, I donate funds to the Torch Foundation and many animal foundations and churches and donate to the building of water wells in Africa, Haiti, and India.

By acknowledging the past, you can improve the future—for yourself and the people and world around you. By intentionally creating a meaningful legacy, you are writing your own history—one where people will acknowledge you for giving and making the world a better place.

**Sacred Words to Use:**

- Historical
- Opportunities
- Inventions
- Lessons
- Achievements
- Education
- Progress

- Legacy
- Advancements
- Traditions
- Discovery
- Recognition
- Awareness
- Legacy

Sacred words and phrases:

- By touring museums, I surround myself with historical reminders of the progresses that have been made throughout time. It's so enriching!

- As part of my legacy, I'm giving back and donating to those who are without basic needs, such as water and shelter.

- The achievements of man are astounding! I acknowledge the technology, inventions, and discoveries that have been made in the past and their role in advancing our life and capabilities.

- In recognition of the work you've done to find a cure for cancer, please accept my donation toward your new research facility.

- Education has played an integral role in my life, and I'm committed to reading a history book every year to enlighten me about our past.

- It is awareness of our past that paves the path to our future. I acknowledge the historical leaders who founded our country, for without them, our country would not be the same.

- Opportunities: The accomplishments throughout history are impressive and plenty—I acknowledge them and those who achieved them for they have opened the door to the opportunities we enjoy today.

- As I make advancements in my life, I acknowledge them with a small reward.

- There is no greater way to acknowledge an invention than to reinvent myself, making improvements as time goes on.

- Every year, I participate in historical traditions, such as reenactments of the Renaissance. It's so educational and interesting!

- The lessons history has taught me are invaluable. As a symbol of my appreciation for their impact on my lives, I share them with my children and grandchildren, passing them down so they will live for centuries to come.

- In acknowledgement of the great work and research that has been done on autism, it is my privilege and honor to donate so research can continue toward finding a cure.

"May your acknowledgement serve the world."

~Margo Majdi

# Homework

- Wherever you are, make it a daily practice to acknowledge at least three people who are your family and/or friends and three more so it becomes your habit and see what unfolds in your life because of it.

- And when someone responds with "Thank you," ask them to refrain of that and receive the acknowledgement, instead of making it an exchange of words.

- Just be aware that people may become uncomfortable when they receive the acknowledgment. So ask them to refrain and to just receive the acknowledgement because a heartfelt acknowledgement gets to be experienced and felt.

- Enjoy seeing others for the masterpieces they are so that you will forever be the change that you wish to see in the world.

- BE EMPOWERING in your life's journey.

*About the Author*

# Margo Majdi

*As the Founder and* President of Mastery in Transformational Training, Margo has supported thousands of people who have dramatically changed their lives by participating in the trainings. She is repeatedly recognized for her work as a leader in the field of transformational trainings and acknowledged by Mayors, Senators, and other dignitaries of the states of California and Massachusetts.

Born and educated in Holland, Margo earned a business degree at age 21. Soon after, she moved to Spain for three years before making her way to America in 1970. Here in the states, she studied Psychology and Re-evaluation Counseling. She owned a successful business in Beverly Hills, a Spa and Beauty Institute.

Her life changed forever in 1980, when she was introduced to transformational trainings. By 1998, she completely transformed her own life by purchasing the rights to the trainings, naming her new company Mastery in Transformational Training (M.I.T.T.).

Through over a decade of networking and expanding, M.I.T.T. has become a leading organization in transformational trainings worldwide, boasting only the most masterful and world-renowned trainers.

Going above and beyond her role as President, Margo spearheads M.I.T.T.'s Leadership Program, through which she has coached thousands of people in creating extraordinary results in their daily lives. Beyond their own lives, she coaches them on focusing their energy outward and into their communities. These participants learn to personally inspire others. They also greatly contribute to the Los Angeles landscape by creating community projects and fundraising millions of dollars for local charitable organizations.

Standing as the example for all of her participants, Margo founded her own charitable organization, The Torch Foundation, which makes transformational trainings accessible to at-risk teenagers throughout Los Angeles and other states. These teens experience huge shifts in their own lives through the trainings and the subsequent month of coaching. For many of them, they are experiencing for the first time what it is like to be responsible and to know that they can make choices toward achieving their dreams. These teens go on to create extraordinary results and become leaders in their schools and communities.

In 2007, Margo brought the Torch Trainings to China. The teen trainings are now amongst the top-rated trainings in China, where they are conducted by the equivalent of Dr. Phil here. They have changed many lives. She is currently working with Dubai to bring the trainings there, and also with the states of Massachusetts, Ohio, and Michigan.

Learn more about Margo Majdi by visiting her website at www.mittraining.com.

Mastery in
Transformational
Training
offers
*The Art of
Acknowledgment* (TM)
workshops so people
can integrate
acknowledgment
in an experiential
training.

To register, go to
www.mittraining.com

Made in the USA
Charleston, SC
04 April 2016